# Memories
# of Singapore and Malaya

# Memories
# of Singapore and Malaya
## by
## Derek Tait

*Best wishes,*

*Derek Tait.*

## Driftwood Coast Publishing

Frontispiece : The Gorilla at Tiger Balm Gardens.

First published 2007

Driftwood Coast Publishing
PO Box 7,West Park,Plymouth,PL5 2YS.
© Derek Tait, 2007

# Contents

# Acknowledgements

Thanks to everyone who contributed memories and photos for this book including John Cunningham, Alan Tait, Ellen Tait, Alan D Tait, Tom O'Brien, Alan Cottrell, Tim Ecott, Andy (Isaac) Newton, Dee Hinton, Kate Spurrier, Geoff Cooper, John Harper, Alan Cooke, Richard Freeman, Colin McCormac, Vivien Webster, Kevin Daley, Clive Baker, David Yap, Peter Banks, Dave Papworth, Lynn McWilliam, Tony Arrowsmith, Steve Burnett, Lisa White, Brian Mitchell and David Robbins. Also thanks to the ANZ Military Brats of Singapore website, run by Jo-Anne Rendle, and all its members for their memories.
Thanks too, to all the people who have contributed to my website over the years. These include Pete Banks, Richard White, Gill Pennock, Ian Hovey, Ian Harris, Kenny Symmons, Ralph Parks, Mike Rendle, Randal McDowell, Colin Bull, Sue Fraser, Lynette Jacques, Marcia Headon, Dennis D. Lund, Dee Hinton, Ric Francis, Anthony Carry, Kayes at PenangTalk, Richard Freeman, Simon Lester, Tim Light, Graham Lamont, Gavin Floyd, Geoff Cooper, Alison McAndie and Don Watson.
I have tried to track down the copyright holders of all photos used and apologise to anyone who hasn't been mentioned.
Check out my website about Singapore and Malaya at :
www.derektait.co.uk/sembawang.html

## Bibliography

Websites:
ANZ Military Brats of Singapore website at:
http://groups.msn.com/ANZMilitaryBratsofSingapore/newhomepage.msnw
Good Morning Yesterday at www.goodmorningyesterday.blogspot.com/
HMS Minerva site at http://www.hmsminerva.info/
Tom O'Brien's Singapore website at www.singas.co.uk
Wikipedia at www.wikipedia.org
Please check out my other books:
Images of England : Plymouth (Tempus 2003).
Plymouth at War (Tempus 2006).
Sampans, Banyans and Rambutans : A Childhood in Singapore and Malaya (Driftwood Coast Publishing 2006).
Saltash Passage (Driftwood Coast Publishing 2007).
Contact me at derek.tait@virgin.net

# Introduction

I'm pleased that my first book about Singapore and Malaya brought back
so many happy memories for people who lived there during the
1950s,1960s and 1970s as part of a Forces family. It made me realise
that there are many other people with fond memories of their time in
Singapore and Malaya so I decided to put together this second edition,
not only featuring more of my memories but also memories of other
people who were there at the same time.
Some of you will have read John Harper's excellent blog on Lam Chun
See's blogsite, 'Good Morning Yesterday', recalling his childhood in
Singapore, and some of it is reproduced here.

John Harper (centre) with his brothers, Tom and Bob.

Also, there are many pictures including Tiger Balm Gardens, downtown
Singapore, Sembawang, HMS Terror, RAF Tengah, school photos,
Amahs Markets, Malaya, Penang etc as well as many more memories
from the people who were there at the time. Other memories come from
Tom O'Brien whose fascinating website recalls all those happy memories
from our time in the Far East.
A lot has changed in Singapore and Malaya over the years and it's always
interesting for me to hear from people who were there at the same time as
I was in the 1960s, who have since returned and noticed many new
buildings, roads and attractions. Our old house and the estate in Johore is
still there, though much more built up. Gone are the miles of jungle which
have been replaced by shopping malls and hotels.

It all seems such a shame now but almost 40 years have passed since we came home so it's not surprising that there have been some changes. I'm sure all of us ex brats would love to return to those warm, sunny days of our childhoods and there probably isn't one of us who doesn't miss it everyday. It seems with the internet, the world is getting smaller. With Google Earth, I can travel to Singapore whenever I want. I've even found our old house and estate nestled amongst the many new high rise buildings. I'm probably not the only one who preferred that time when there were no internet or emails, or other modern technology, when the world seemed a lot bigger place and we all made our own entertainment. I'm always amazed to hear from people who were there at the same time as me who are now tv presenters, airline pilots, estate agents, businessmen etc. How did we all get so old? I still feel like that little kid sat on the beach on Jason's Bay all that time ago. My only worry then was probably missing an episode of Samurai!

I hope this new compilation will jog many people's memories and thanks to all the people who have contributed and helped to keep the memory alive.

My first book on Singapore and Malaya is now in 40 libraries in Singapore as well as in the library at Dalat School in Penang which was once Sandycroft Leave Centre. So, if you contributed to this edition, it may well be the case that someone you knew in the Far East gets to read it.

I'm still looking for my father's friend, Poon, who was stationed at KD Malaya at the Woodlands Base at Sembawang in Singapore. If anyone knows his whereabouts nowadays, please contact me. Or if you just want to reminisce about the old days, please contact me also.

Whatever you're doing now, whether you're retired, an airline pilot, an office worker etc, stop what you're doing and spend a while reliving the good old days...

# One
## Leaving England

Being only three years old when we left England, I remember little about it, although I have early memories of living in Weymouth. All our possessions were packed away and put into storage in England for three years. Unfortunately, by the time we returned, some of it had disappeared forever!

My family in England in the 1960s before we made the trip to Singapore. It was Guy Fawkes night and someone has put a monkey in my pram. Those were the days when you would see monkeys at fairgrounds and pier fronts etc. I wonder if they were cousins of the ones in the Botanic Gardens? It looks like I was pretty wary of them even then!

My dad was seconded to the Malayan Navy to work at KD Malaya, within the Naval Base at Woodlands in Sembawang. My parents were 29 and my brother was 8 years old. We left England on 24th January 1965. It was the first time I'd ever been abroad and my first time travelling on an aeroplane. I couldn't have imagined how different Singapore and Malaya would have been from my world in Weymouth but what an opportunity to travel to almost the other side of the world and to live there for three years. It was an adventure for me and my brother Alan but my parents were probably very apprehensive about leaving England and living in another country. Strangely enough, we must have had lots of injections before we left but I don't remember any of them. The later ones in Singapore, and the sore arms that came with them, stick in my mind though!

**Kevin Daley remembers:**
**Prior to arriving in Singapore, I will always remember the chat that my uncle gave to both myself and my older brother. My uncle served his National Service with the Argyll and Southerland Highlanders and was familiar with the events of the Malayan Communist uprising and its Guerrilla war against the Malayan and British administration. Apparently, we were likely to be in many precarious situations and we always had to keep our wits about us. Given the chance 'they' would take us behind a building and slit our throats. Crikey!**
**I recall wondering if my Dad's draft to Singapore was a form of punishment for some misdemeanour he had committed, somewhat like being sent to Australia along with all the other convicts.**
**I am sure my uncle's chat was designed to keep us on our toes and to be ever alert but his words were always fresh in my mind before heading east and I recall my brother and I mulling over the imminent dangers we would face as the date of departure got ever nearer.**
**It was during this time that I felt there were more negatives than positives with anything to do with Malaya and Singapore. This feeling was compounded by the constant visits made to the doctor's surgery to be peppered by injections from a battery of diligent nurses. There seemed to be a lot of nasty things that had the potential to kill us apart from the 'natives'. Once again I wondered what bad deed my father must have done to receive this harsh a punishment!**

**John Harper remembers:**
**For many, this was a hectic time. You received the information booklet about Singapore giving you a load of information about the country with do's and don'ts, which made interesting reading, but in**

no way could it fully prepare you for what you were going to experience. For many, the trauma of injections and inoculations was to follow. The TABT injection against typhoid was particularly painful. Many have described the painful swollen arm. For our family, the timing of the injections meant that the second injection was given on the ship as we sailed for Singapore. My younger brothers were given an adult dose through a miscalculation by the Army doctor on the ship and ended up bed ridden for a few days unable to move.

As service families, you usually didn't have many possessions, being ready to move sometimes at extremely short notice. However, there were items of clothing and some personal belongings to be packed. Some for storage whilst abroad and some to go with you to Singapore. Many children would see their toys going into storage for the duration of the stay abroad. Some toys were even given away! But this was often offset by the anticipation of moving to somewhere very different.

A pupil going abroad was a teaching opportunity for many teachers. Out would come the atlas and a look at the world map to show how far away the pupil was going. I think that to many people, back in those days, where many people travelled no further than the coast for a seaside holiday, it was impossible to comprehend what a long journey it was going to be. This was particularly true for those travelling by ship and even more so when the ships had to go round the Cape at the time of the Suez crisis. Even the journey by air took several days, compare that with the 11-hour journey of today between Heathrow and Singapore.

The year was 1957. We had lived in Cleveleys near Blackpool for nearly five years, whilst my father was posted to RAF Weeton, and it had almost felt as though we were putting down permanent roots. It was sometime just before my tenth birthday. My mother gathered my brothers Tom, Bob and me together one weekend, when my father had got home from working on Saturday morning, and my father announced that he had been posted to Singapore and that we would be following him out there a couple of months after he went. My father was a man of few words and left my mother to go through the booklet on Singapore with us. She explained where it was, beyond India but not as far as China and near the equator, the small diamond shaped island that looks like it is about to be swallowed by the snake head of Malaya. It was going to be warm but the air would be very moist and there would be quite a lot of rain. Later, I read that booklet from cover to cover for myself and although I can't remember much of what was in there, I do remember thinking what a different exciting sort of place it seemed to be. After my father left, the next few months were going to prove a very trying time for my mother. She had to manage the packing up of everything we owned after sorting what was to come with us and what was to go into storage.

There were injections and inoculations, some of them very painful. We had to travel from Cleveleys to RAF Weeton for the Yellow Fever injection but the rest could be done by our local GP. On the way for the smallpox inoculation at the local GPs, my brother Tom tripped over a kerbstone and broke his elbow. So, as well as coping with the injection, he had to cope with the pain of a broken elbow. The doctor advised putting his arm in a sling and waiting until the morning before going to Victoria hospital to get it x-rayed and seen to. So, that was the following day taken away from my mother's preparations to move. As the arm had swollen overnight, it wasn't put into plaster and he arrived home with it bound to his chest in a tight sling with lots of padding around the elbow. The preparations continued, friends and teachers were told of our forthcoming move, I don't think that most of them could comprehend moving half way round the world to another country.

At last, my brother Tom's arm was given the all clear and brought back into full use just two weeks before we were leaving. Unfortunately, this wasn't to be the last disaster before we moved. A week later, I was playing cricket in the school yard at lunchtime. A ball came past me and I gave chase only to bump into somebody who turned round just as I got up speed, head down following the ball. Over I went with a sickening crunch landed on my wrist, sustaining a fracture to my left wrist. I knew it was broken from the pain and the strange bowed appearance that looked like the broken right wrist I had sustained about eighteen months before, piggy back fighting in the same school yard. One of the dinner ladies took me home and insisted that she take me on to the hospital so that mum could get on with the final preparations for moving. So, mum gladly but nonetheless feeling slightly guilty, wrote a letter of authority for the dinner lady to act in loco-parentis and off we went on the tram to Blackpool to the Victoria hospital.

The letter proved useful as, of course, permission for me to have the bone set under anaesthetic was necessary. Coming back on the tram, with my arm in plaster, I suddenly felt sick and had to leave the tram for some fresh air. We walked one stop along and then got on the next tram that came.

# Two

# The Journey

Our journey was long to Singapore, about 16 hours. The plane stopped at Karachi, in Pakistan, to refuel. When the plane doors opened, we were hit by the awful smell and the intense heat. I'm told that I still had my Winter clothes on from England because I'd refused to change them. I must have been pretty hot by then!

While on the plane, the Captain announced that Winston Churchill had died. Seems like a long, long time ago now.

It must have seemed a very long journey for a three year old. I probably slept through a lot of it though.

**John Harper remembers:**
**At last, leaving day arrived. The two old ladies across the road came over to say goodbye and gave us a large bar of chocolate for the journey. We felt a little bit guilty as we had always called them the 'mad ladies' because they had complained when we had lost balls in their garden. Many of the neighbours came to say goodbye and we were pleasantly surprised to see how many people had turned out**

just to bid us farewell. We went to one of the Blackpool stations, I think it was the central one, and got on a train and eventually ended up in London where we were then taken by bus to the Union Jack club for an overnight stay. Next day, after lunch, we were taken to Waterloo station and put on a boat train to Southampton. We shared the train compartment with a Glaswegian family and although it was difficult to understand what they were saying at first, my ears tuned in after a while and life stories were swapped. As the train arrived, my mother got me to put a Macintosh over my arm to hide the plaster, as she wasn't sure whether we would be allowed to travel if anyone spotted it. To make doubly sure, my brothers and the Glaswegian family, we were sharing the train carriage with, surrounded me to further hide the arm.

Before us was what looked to me like a magnificent liner, the S.S. Dilwara. I had never been this close to such a large ship before. Trawlers in Fleetwood harbour and steamers on Lake Windermere had been the largest things that I had seen. After our documentation had been checked, we all trooped up the gangway with all the children, still crowding round me to hide the arm in plaster. Once on board, I was confined to the cabin until we had set sail, and were well away from the port, before I was allowed out.

As it turned out, my mother's instincts had been correct as the M.O. said that I shouldn't have been allowed on board with my arm in plaster. Despite that, he did arrange for the plaster to be removed at an Army base when we arrived in Mauritius. Life on board a ship with your arm in plaster was an interesting experience as a young lad. At first, I was a little bit cautious but I quickly adjusted and almost became unaware that the arm was in plaster. I think that a few of us must have been just about all over that ship, including areas that were marked out of bounds for passengers. It was great fun for a young lad and we never got caught although it was a close call sometimes.

Meals on board were always signalled with a bell and there was always a great stampede to get to the dining room. Most children would be running and would do a hurdle-style jump through the step of the bulkhead door leading into the dining room. In the Bay of Biscay, the ship was rolling quite violently from side to side, the bell rang and instinct took over with the usual rush amongst those that had good sea legs and were not confined to their cabin with seasickness. Leaping over the bulkhead step, the ship rolled and the angle of the step came up to meet my trajectory and over I went completing my entry into the dining room with a sprawling somersault. Somehow, I managed to hold my plaster cast arm out of the way and fortunately, no damage was done. How nobody was ever hurt in that three times daily stampede, I'll never understand. We were soon out of the Bay of Biscay and heading to warmer latitudes. A couple of days each week, a part of the deck would be flooded as a shallow swimming pool and paddling pool so that we could cool off. To make use of this, my mother used to bind my plaster cast up in a plastic bag with sellotape. It was not particularly comfortable with the plastic bag and also trying to keep the plaster away from any inadvertent ingress of water but that cooling dip in the water was well worth it.

As we passed round Africa, our first stop was in Dakar to take on fuel. I can't remember much about Dakar except that the stop was short and we didn't even leave the ship. The next stop was Cape Town where we were taken off the ship and went for a bus tour of Cape Town and Table Mountain. On returning to the ship, mum bought some extremely large pears. Half a pear was enough and I swear they were the sweetest juiciest flavoursome pears that I have ever tasted. I'm drooling just thinking about the juice dribbling down my chin!

Malcolm and Ian Younger broke out in a rash, I can't remember whether it was measles or Chicken Pox, after a few days on the ship and were confined to a quarantine cabin situated near the back of the ship underneath the lifting gear. On nice days, they were allowed to come out and look down enviously at the rest of us having fun. It wasn't until they got out of quarantine that we got to know them and found out why they were up there. We all thought that they must be an important family with a special cabin! Malcolm and I became fairly good friends during that time and at Changi we lived in the same road for some time and were in the same class at school. By chance, as well, when we returned to the UK, the Younger family arrived back a few days after us and were staying in the same transit boarding house in Blackpool, where we both attended Blackpool Grammar School in the same class again. We both hated that school with a vengeance but that's another story.

From Cape Town, we headed up into the Indian Ocean heading towards Mauritius which was to be our next stop. Part way there, a load of activity took place, with removal of the hold covers and testing of the lifting gear. We had also changed direction. The Tannoy system boomed out that we were diverting to pick up an injured seaman from another ship who needed urgent medical attention. Half a day later, it was announced that another ship had got there before us and that we would be returning to our previous course.

Arriving in Port Louis was an interesting event. The whole port area had an awful smell and we nicknamed it Port Pooey. The following morning, I left the ship with my mother to be met by an Army ambulance on the dockside. We seemed to drive for hours and hours through mile after mile of sugar cane and up towards the mountains. I suspect that it was only about a half hour, it just seemed longer in the back of an ambulance with nothing to see except mile after mile of sugar cane. A recent visit to Mauritius has confirmed my memory of vast expanses of sugar cane.

The plaster cast was, by now, only loosely covering my arm which had shrunk with sweating and the muscles wasting away. When the M.O. got the snippers out to remove it, I told him there was no need and just slipped the cast off over my fingers. The arm was duly x- rayed to confirm that the break had healed okay. Despite the healed bone, the M.O. said that he was not going to take a chance with a young lad travelling on a ship getting into mischief and re-breaking the arm. One of the biggest disappointments was to have a new cast put on before being put back into the ambulance and taken back to Port Louis and the ship. Arrangements were then made for the removal of the cast when we arrived at RAF Changi in Singapore. In the meantime, all the other children had been taken off to a beach somewhere for the day. For many years, I felt jealous of my brothers, Bob and Tom, that they had been taken to an exotic beach somewhere. I only found out a couple of months ago that the person who was looking after them, whilst my mother and I went to have the plaster cast seen to, made them sit under the trees in the shade and wouldn't allow them to go anywhere near the water. Jealous feelings immediately extinguished. I probably had just as interesting a time of it as they had, even if was only looking at mile after mile of sugar cane.

From Mauritius to Singapore, time seemed to drag. I lay in my bunk at night hearing the persistent throb throb throb of the engines. Even watching the porpoise and flying fish had become boring. It was almost routine to look over the side to see if there were any fish or porpoise. It felt like we were trapped on the S.S. Dilwara and it was hardly moving, with us never to see land again. It may not have been the Marie Celeste, too many people on board, but the slowness of that last part of the journey must come a close second to forever sailing round the world. The novelty of being on board a ship had worn thin and it was a great relief when we finally entered the Straits of Malacca and we could see land nearby. Suddenly, the voyage had become exciting again with just one day to go. We made our way down the coast of Malaya overnight and docked in Singapore harbour in the morning. As the ship was docking, I could see my father standing on the dockside. He looked different in Khaki Drill shorts as I had only ever seen him in his UK Air Force Blue uniform. We disembarked and were led to a bus that then took us to the Tanah Merah Country Club where we were treated to a Coca Cola. This was my first taste of the drink and it was to become a firm favourite during our stay. Another favourite was the Sarsaparilla that they sold in the NAAFI. After the drink, it was back on to the bus and not long after, we arrived at Lloyd Leas married quarters. We had finally arrived after having set off from England six weeks before. Within a few days, my plaster cast was removed and we could get down to the serious business of getting acclimatised and getting to know people. The broken arm disasters were not over yet. We had only been at Lloyd Leas a few weeks when my youngest brother, Bob, was outside playing when he fell over a dog and broke his arm. In those days, my mother felt that her second home was the hospital! Despite the setbacks though, we were glad that we had arrived and were settled into a nice bungalow.

Singapore airport 1960s.

Singapore Airport was based at Payer Lebar which was built as a civilian airport in 1955. Eventually, the airport got too small for all the air traffic it was receiving and a new airport was built at Changi in 1975 which opened in 1981.
Most of us arriving at Singapore in the 1960s though would have landed at Payer Lebar and this would have been our first experience of the Far East.

# Three
# Arriving

When we arrived in Singapore by plane, it was early dawn. Everything was lit up, it looked quite different to England. There was a pink glow to the sky and there seemed to be more stars in the sky than we ever saw at home.

We were met by Bob Beaman, an Australian, who was also seconded to KD Malaya, and taken to The Straits Hotel which was along the Skudai in Johore Bahru. We stayed there for a while until we found a place to rent.

**Kevin Daley remembers:**
**I will always remember my first experience of our night time arrival in Singapore. The door of the aircraft was opened and everyone onboard was taken aback by the high heat and humidity that hit us as we sat in our seats. It wasn't too long before I forgot about the cramped conditions onboard and lengthy flight and I yearned to return to the cool interior of the Bristol Britannia aircraft.**

Lynn McWilliam in Singapore Airport,1965

**Brian Mitchell remembers:**
**Music was, of course, important to us young teenagers and I recall hanging around the jukebox in the hotel we stayed at on arrival in Singapore (called The Ambassador and near the site of what used to be Singapore's original airport at Kallang) playing Everly Brothers, Buddy Holly and Elvis records.**

18

David Robbins remembers:
After we had settled down, it was time to deal with the practical matters of entering a new country. We had no local money. The currency of Singapore was Straits Dollars and there was a money changing kiosk at the main entrance. We exchanged what English money we had and studied the notes and coins that we had been given. They felt and looked very old, the coins had so much lettering and we had no idea of their worth. The small brass coins were an odd shape too, we were fascinated.

Singapore Airport 1960s.

With our luggage on the trolley, with us all holding each other's hands, we left the airport terminal and boarded a white bus bearing the lettering 'Seletar Bus Company', which took us to the centre of early morning tropical Singapore. We travelled a few miles from Changi into the city centre, enchanted by our surroundings. On either side of the narrow street were open fronted stores with stacks of their wares out in front. Rickshaw drivers weaved in and out of the traffic. Old trucks, carrying so many workers that they looked like they would overturn and spill onto the road, manoeuvred amongst taxis and pedestrians. Weather beaten Chinese men rode bicycles, overloaded with the goods they were carrying to market. Palm trees lined the wider avenues that brought us to the Seven Storey Hotel, where we were going to spend the day and night at before travelling North to our destination of Seremban, two hundred miles away up country.

After settling into our hotel rooms, we walked up to the restaurant on the top floor of our hotel. From the window, next to our breakfast table, I watched a Malay man performing his morning meditation on the roof of the building next to the hotel. In the distance, the sound calling Muslim people to their temple, travelled over the roofs and through the louvered glass, where we sat eating fresh pineapple and papaya. The voice calling Muslims to prayer was an exotic backdrop to our meal and created a feeling in me like we were part of a film. When we were finished with breakfast, we went back to our rooms to change into clothes suitable for a walk around the waterfront. We put on shorts and sandals and the lightest clothes we owned. As we walked downstairs, dad told us that we were going to have to buy new clothing as soon as we arrived at our new house in the garrison of Seremban. We had brought light clothes in anticipation of the tropical climate but we were unprepared for the heat.

The air outside was thick with humidity and smells from all the stores around the street level in front of the hotel. Spices and salted meat, oriental vegetables that we had never seen before and noisy hawkers selling everything from watches to live chickens. We walked toward the quayside and watched a tiny Malay man cook fried rice in a wok over a flame in a cup. The smell was enticing. A few yards away, a tattooist worked on a man's back, laboriously etching a large dragon onto his skin by hand. This was Collyer Quay. Street vendors and pirates were the constant denizens of this part of the Singapore waterfront. A man in a sarong, checked shirt and fez hat, approached us with his shirt sleeve pulled back. He showed us a forearm sporting at least thirty watches.

'Only fi' dollar, Johnny!' he shouted.

We ignored him and he immediately accosted a couple walking behind us with the same proposition.

All this was like a dream sequence to me. I had landed in the pages of a novel and I was eager to keep reading. From every store, we could hear music which included high pitched Tamil singing, Chinese pop and the Beatles. They all blended into a wonderful symphony of sound that accompanied our surreal walk along the quayside.

A warm breeze floated off the water as we crossed the street and wandered into Change Alley, a street market squeezed between tall, old buildings. It was almost noon and the stalls were closing for the afternoon. We wanted to buy flip flops but we were too late. Dad asked a tiny, rugged looking woman, wearing what I thought were pyjamas, when the market would reopen.

'Dark, Johnny!' she said, while wrestling with a large canvas tarpaulin that she was dragging over her table. We took this to mean that we would have to wait until after sunset.

We ambled back along Collyer Quay to our hotel, without buying flip flops, starting to feel tired from the heavy, close air. The breeze direction had shifted and was bringing the strong pungent aroma of tropical low tide onto the land. Most of the shops were closed, or about to be, and we were glad to step inside the air conditioned Seven Storey. Up in our rooms on the fourth floor, we lay down for a nap, listening again to the voice of the man calling Muslims to prayer at a nearby mosque.

Dad woke us all so we could go for a walk and explore. We met up with Simon and mum outside their room and took the elevator down to the ground floor.

'The elevator goes up eight floors!' John remarked. 'Why do they call this the Seven Storey Hotel?'

'Maybe they don't count the same here!' Anthony replied.

We all laughed and Dad told him that was a good a reason as any he could think of!

Outside, Singapore was waking up from the hot afternoon. Beside the wide road following the quayside, a long row of market stalls was setting up. Some were already open and we all wandered along in the early evening light, looking for flip flops. We found and bought a pair each and put them on straight away. It wasn't long before the sun went down, faster than I had ever seen. Without being asked, John explained that we were so close to the Equator that there was no real sunset.

We visited the busy Amah's market. The humidity was much lighter now and very comfortable. The temperature was perfect. A light breeze carried the evening scents of fried rice, roasting pork, incense and all the aromas of the waterfront.

By this time, we had walked to the end of the Amah's market and were a long way from our hotel. We were hungry and the cooking and the smells from the street market were very strong but we were wary of buying and eating any food that was being prepared in those street side conditions. It was time to go back to the Seven Storey Hotel for dinner. Turning back along the quayside, we walked to the seawall and watched the lights of the ferry boats leaving the piers and crossing the Straits of Singapore to islands that were no more than shadows across the water.

Dad saw a taxi and whistled to get the driver's attention. The old Mercedes, with an air conditioning unit protruding from a rear window, stopped beside us and the turbaned man behind the wheel leaned over and said something in a language I had never heard

**before. Dad leaned in the window and handed the man a dollar. Then, suddenly, the cab driver spoke English.**
**'Downtown, Johnny?' he asked.**
**'Seven Storey!' Dad answered.**
**'Eight Storey!' muttered John as we all climbed into the car.**

David Robbins tale about the Seven Storey Hotel reminds me of when we were backpacking around Australia in 1990 and we stopped off in Singapore for 10 days on the way back. We had to book a cheap hotel, as we didn't have much money, so we wrote to a few from Australia. The only one good enough to reply was the 7th Storey Hotel (which I think must be the Seven Storey Hotel in David's account) so we stayed there for several days. When we got to Singapore and told the taxi driver where we were staying he said, 'You don't want to stay there - it's very old!' We had to though as we were running out of money! When we got to the hotel, it was covered in bamboo scaffolding poles. Our room was sparse but the staff had left out a pair of flip flops for us. One was a size 10 and the other was a size 5! The staff were friendly enough but the hotel had seen better days. I'm sure it couldn't have changed much since the 1960s. In the morning, after being woken by cockroaches, we got the lift to the top floor where the restaurant was. We seemed to be the only guests staying there, though there was a colour leaflet showing people disco dancing at night in the restaurant. I'm sure it was from the 1970s. It had a great view over the city but I think we only stayed another night before moving to the luxurious YMCA on Orchard Road which was unlike the YMCAs here and more like a 5 star hotel.
Anyway below is a picture of the 7th Storey Hotel restaurant and also those afore mentioned disco dancers!

The 7th Storey Hotel.
Many of us stayed here on arrival in Singapore in the 1960s and again
when we left.

# Four
# Our New Homes

Our new home from 1965 was at 103 Jalan Wijaya at Century Gardens in Johore Bahru in Malaya. It was a newly built estate and we had a small semi detached bungalow.

We lived there for the next 3 years. We had a Chinese landlord to start with, Yap Choon Lim, but he sold it to Swan Singh ,who was a Sikh, and his brothers. I can remember one was called Dajet Singh but there were about 5 others. Swan Singh was very friendly. He wore shoes with turned up toes and a turban. He was well over 6ft tall. He used to buy us chocolate if he saw us at the Cold Store.

I loved it at Jalan Wijaya. If we weren't playing in the garden, we'd be wandering around the estate either going to the shops or looking for materials to build dens. I have more memories of our time spent at home than I have at school but school days seemed relatively short compared to the ones back in England.

Everyone we seemed to see regularly lived nearby or on adjoining estates.

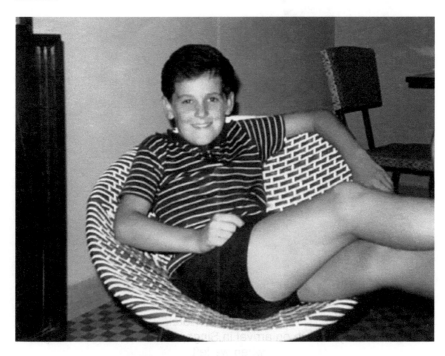

My brother, Alan, in our front room.

Here's a photo of my mum with our front doors in the background. Across the road was a row of shops which included an insurance sales man who had a monkey chained outside. There was also a cold store which I remember for all the free gifts you got whenever you purchased something. These included free buckets with washing powder and free tea sets with tea and coffee. Incidentally, this is the first photo I ever took, not bad for a three year old!

My mum and me in our garden.

Here's proof that I never missed the daily visit by the ice cream van even if I was having a bath at the time! Someone else had to queue up for me. The ice cream man, complete with turban, would come on a scooter which had his small van attached.

My brother, Alan, outside our home in his sea cadets uniform. The cadets were based at HMS Terror.

Me and my brother, Alan, at our home in Jalan Wijaya on my sixth
birthday. Look at that great cake!

Our post was delivered by a cheery Indian, he'd ring the bell on his bike
until we took the mail from him. We loved getting letters from our Gran in
Sunderland as she used to put sweets or sherbet dabs in them! The
sherbet probably wouldn't get through customs now! I think we missed the
English sweets, though they must have been on sale in Singapore. The
Chinese sweets were inedible to us.
My dad had a reel to reel tape recorder and we'd all record messages on
it and send it back to my Gran and she would let us know what she was
up to and send one back. I wish I had all of those tapes now. I remember
one message we recorded was when we had just come back from Tiger
Balm Gardens and another was when we returned from Johore Zoo.
Malaya must have seemed a world a way from Seaham Harbour!
Birthdays were a great time and all the kids from the estate would come
over with presents. The toys were so fantastic there that you'd always get
something good. These would include tin robots, cars and planes etc, all
battery operated. The toys seemed ingenious then.
Being near Johore Bahru, we were close to many attractions including
Kota Tinghi Waterfalls, the zoo and Jason's Bay.
There always seemed to be something going on. On Chinese New Year,

27

there would be fireworks and fire crackers going off everywhere though home firework displays seemed to be a regular occurrence. My dad, or one of his friends, would always be having a barbeque and we'd sit out on warm nights under the stars listening to all the crickets and the frogs and toads in the storm drains.

My mum and dad at a party at our house. I would have been tucked up in bed fast asleep probably. I remember that my dad won that ice bucket in a raffle at the Navy Base!

Kevin Daley remembers:
I felt we all settled into our first few weeks in Malaya pretty well.
Once we were over the jet-lag, and the local mosquito population
had added our tastes to their onboard database, we were ready to
experience our new world. Going to school was okay as we always
finished early in the afternoon. This meant that most days we could
go swimming, fishing or shopping to buy the items we needed for
life in a tropical climate. One of the strangest early experiences we
had was going to the market area in JB and having to strip to our
underwear as various styles and colours of shorts and shirts were
aimed our way. Sandals and flip-flops were the order of the day but I
remember that bare feet seemed to be the norm around the house
and in our garden. Having said that, we were always cautious
watching out for the black boot-lace snakes that we were warned
would be the most likely cause of a snake bite. In our two and a half
years in Malaya and Singapore, I never did see one of those mythical
snakes. However, sighting King Cobras nesting in the garden, water
snakes, sea snakes and pythons seemed to be a weekly occurrence.

Kevin Daley remembers:
5 Jalan Giam, December 1966. Our new home in Malaya. Within a
short walk, we had open ground where I used to catch Atlas moths.
To the right is where a family of Chinese lived. We used to play with
the daughters. To the left is where the Beatty family lived and behind
us were the shops which included a tropical fish shop.
Our bungalow in Jalan Giam was on quite a large plot and we had
banana trees growing at the rear along with bamboo plants. Along
the fence by the driveway, a large creeper grew which provided year

29

round flowers. This plant was a magnet for absolutely enormous bees. My older brother, Ray, and I soon developed a game of dare which involved closing the large pink and white petals around the body of a bee. As soon as the bee realised that it was trapped it went into a buzzing frenzy and the aim of the game was to see who would dare to maintain a grip on the flower the longest. Over the course of what must have been several months, we both became quite expert at creating a range of buzzing melodies and other friends we had visit would stare in disbelief as we practised our skill. I have to point out that we never once harmed the bees inside and more often than not they would go about their nectar collecting chores as soon as they were released. Anyway, our game of dare was soon to become a thing of the past when I was stung on the thumb by a very irate bee. Within seconds my thumb had swollen to such an extent that it looked like I had large yam instead of a thumb. Lesson learnt. Bees = 1, KD = 0!

Kevin Daley remembers:
December 1966. Fred is still very much a puppy here. He couldn't have been smuggled over the border too long when this photo was taken.

Ellen Tait remembers: We were never burgled but this happened to a few people. We had windows, with fancy steel bars, which meant you could leave them open at night but nobody could get in.  However, the burglars  would get a long bamboo pole, attach a hook to the end and put it through the slats and hook trousers to take money from them! Any small items that could be hooked disappeared!
The house opposite was owned by a Mr Lee and family. He had two wives, an older one and a younger one. He asked me over one night and I met  Tunka Abdul Rahman, the first prime minister of Malaysia.

The Daley Family keeping cool in March 1967.

Kevin Daley remembers:
We were based at Rosyth before we went to Malaya. We left with deep snow on the ground. I always remember trying to tell our Malayan friends about snow but they couldn't grasp it. Try explaining snow to someone that has never seen it. It was a bit like trying to describe air.

Tim Ecott remembers:
The smells of Malaya have stayed in my memory most. Things like the frangipani blossoms, after the monsoon rains, and the car always having the gluey 'stink' of the green paper umbrellas that we always took in case we got caught in a downpour. My sister and I would dare each other to sniff the durians and the shops were always full of little wisps of smoke from all the joss sticks.

Swimming was a daily activity and I remember my sister's hair turning slightly green from the chlorine in the pool. My friends and I played at being soldiers a lot and, because we were in the Far East, the enemy was always the Japanese. We were fuelled by constant supplies of Commando comics. Our dads got the camp tailor to make us little uniforms, but we had no control over what rank we got. I was made a Corporal but my friend Bobby was a Sergeant so he was always allowed to boss me around. Then, a new boy came from New Zealand and his Dad made him an officer, something that caused quite an upset with the other parents! We allowed him to be our leader and he would make us eat tablespoonfuls of salt to 'protect us from dehydration when we were on a jungle mission'.

Going shopping with Mum was always fun, because the shopkeepers plied us with cold drinks and sweets and I loved going to the market in Taiping. Once, we were allowed to buy some day old chicks. They all died within a few days except for one and he grew into a massive cockerel that terrorized our three dogs and eventually became so fierce that no-one could go into the back garden without being chased.

There wasn't much on TV but I remember the Ninja programme and our gang making 'fighting stars' out of coke cans. They seemed quite dangerous at the time but I don't think they could be thrown very far. My other favourite was Flipper.

In Taiping the best place was the New Club where there were swimming pools carved into the rocks and fed by mountain streams. We could always hear the gibbons making their sad whoop-whooping cries while we swam in the cool dark water.

In KL, we were taken on an excursion to the Batu Caves where you had to slither down a rope into the caves and there were thousands of bats living on the ceiling. It was a big adventure but the strongest memory is of a five legged cow that was kept as a curiosity in a field outside the caves. The leg was quite normal but it grew out of the cow's back and dangled down.

Sometimes, as a treat, I was allowed to buy a stuffed snake and once I bought a stuffed monitor lizard which lasted for about twenty years until the legs started cracking and letting the stuffing out. The best curio was a stuffed mongoose fighting a cobra and I kept in my bedroom back in the UK for years.

All of the kids lived in flip-flops and I once ran across the lawn and tripped into the big monsoon ditch. Whenever we fell over, my Dad always screamed 'those bloody flip-flops' and for once he was right. He had to take me to the clinic to get stitches in my head and my knee and I still have the scars!

Lynne McWilliam and her dad outside their house at Prince Edward Park.

**Kevin Daley remembers:**
**Our local friends always wanted to borrow my Mum and Dad's**
**records to learn how to play the tunes. It was fun to hear them learn**
**various Rolling Stones and Animals songs. In return, we used to get**
**invited to their village for a meal. I was always amazed to find out**
**that everything that involved meat would have been slaughtered and**
**prepared that day. I also found it strange to have to make up your**
**own meal from lots of different individual dishes. There were no**
**ready assembled meals like Nasi Goreng. Most of the dishes were**
**unrecognisable but I am still here so there couldn't have been**
**anything too bad. The taste for hot and spicy food is still a favourite**
**of mine today.**

**Kevin Daley remembers: Our dog, Fred, in 1967. We were never sure why Fred barked at all the locals. It may be that he saw too many dogs being taken into the jungle with plastic buckets over their heads!**

Like Kevin, I remember all the dogs that wandered around the estate. Unfortunately, most ended up being shot by the police because of the fear that they would attack someone or because they might have rabies. Many of the kids played with the dogs and my brother was bitten by one. He wasn't too happy because he had to have a tetanus shot and he hated needles. There were certainly many dogs roaming about and I remember being worried by them. One stood up on my shoulders and licked me and that was enough to have me running all the way home!

There weren't many dangers though from wandering the estate. There was little traffic, especially down our street, and most people knew each other. All the kids were out and about playing on their bikes or go karts. the world seemed a lot safer place back then and I don't really remember any trouble.

Probably the biggest danger was falling into a monsoon drain but even those who did lived to tell the tale. You were probably more likely to need hospital treatment from the muck down there than you were from the fall. Some kids even played in the drains but there were warnings about some of the things you could catch. I heard about an unpleasant worm that was meant to get into your system. Most storm drains consisted of old soggy cardboard, dead animals, including dogs and chickens, and beer cans.

**Lynn McWilliam remembers:**
**Here's a photo of TV Singapura with the news reader. We thought that it was normal to have only one TV channel in those days. I remember when we moved to Prince Edward Park, we could also get TV Malaya. Star Trek was on Sunday afternoon on Singapura and Sunday evening on TV Malaya. What bliss!**

I remember watching my favourite show, Samurai, on a tv like this. There wasn't a kid in Australia, Japan or Singapore who hadn't seen Samurai. Yet, when we got back to England, nobody had heard of it. Samurai starred Koichi Ose, who was a top movie star in Japan at the time. He played the lead character, Shintaro. His arch enemies were the Koga Ninjas.
Samurai was a huge show and when Koichi Ose visited Australia in the 1960s, he got a bigger welcome than the Beatles. He was greeted by screaming fans in home made kimonos throwing Ninja stars made of cardboard. Apparently, he had no idea how popular he was outside Japan.
The show ran throughout the 1960s having first been shown in Japan in 1962. It was dubbed into English which could be quite funny some times. For instance, Shintaro would be giving a long speech and his mouth would be moving quite a lot and the dubbed voice would just say something like, 'Yes, I know'.
Samurai had us all making five pointed Ninja stars out of Coke tins. Coke tins were a lot thicker then and the metal used was ideal for making Ninja stars. They were probably quite deadly but I can't remember anyone getting hurt.
Incidentally, Koichi Ose is still alive and living in Japan. He retired in 1969 and started up a property company and in 1980, he and his wife opened a chain of noodle restaurants. I hope he has as fond memories as I have of Samurai.

**Ellen Tait remembers: We hired a TV  and, when we had it on, the local children would sit on the gate and watch it through the open doors! I think that's where we first saw Star Trek.**
**The programmes were hilarious. A prize in a quiz show was described as, 'A lawn mower - just the thing for lawn mowing!'. They also had talent shows but they all came out and sang the same song, 'I went to your wedding', which was popular at the time but we grew to hate it! On another night they would all sing, 'Fly me to the Moon' and we were wishing they would, they were terrible!**

Television didn't start until 1963 in Singapore so not all of us got to see it. By the time we got there in 1965,most of the programmes I remember were American like I Dream of Jeannie, Bewitched, The Flintstones, Lost in Space, Time Tunnel, Voyage to the Bottom of the Sea, Hogan's Heroes, F Troop and Zorro. All of these were popular with both adults and kids. The children's programmes included Gigantor, Marine Boy and Flipper. I can't remember ever watching the news but it must have been on.

**Brian Mitchell remembers:**
**We had no television when we first arrived in Singapore and the radio was difficult to listen to in the evening with all the static from electric storms. I enjoyed the cartoons in the Straits Times which included strips from the United States including Lil' Abner. We also enjoyed Dick Tracy and Mad Magazine was much looked forward to, although this featured satires on US tv programmes none of which I had even seen!**

**Kevin Daley remembers:**
**A typical outcome of a downpour in the monsoon season. No respite from the heat and tons of humidity added for comfort.**

This photo really captures what it was like after a downpour. The ground was wet but it was still very warm and humid. I can almost smell what it was like from this picture. Singapore and Malaya had a smell all of its own but it was certainly different when it rained! Sometimes the storm drains would flood and the water would come up to our front door. I never remember it coming in the house which is probably just as well with all the stuff that must have been down there. I loved the heavy rain, it cooled everything down even though the rain itself seemed to be warm. The downpours never seemed to last for long and the sun was soon out again.

**Ellen Tait remembers: The weather was very hot and humid most of the time. When the Monsoon season came, it was heaven! We use to stand out in the rain splashing around just to cool down. The Amah thought we were mad as she was so cold.**

The Daley family outside their house on their way to the Naval Base pool in December 1966. Look at that lovely car!

**Debbie Hynd remembers:**
**I remember a chit chat falling off the roof into my mother's cup of Milo. I also remember a chit chat running in between my sisters toes when she had her sandals on and her screaming her head off. There was also the skeleton of a chit chat painted onto our window sill and chit chats fell onto the mosquito nets above the beds. Thank God for those mossy nets!**

Chit chats seemed to be everywhere in our home. We loved watching them outside running up and down the walls and were fascinated when they ran off leaving behind their tails. Because the doors and windows were often open, many of them made their way indoors which meant you had to check your bed every night. They seemed to love anywhere warm and quiet. They loved all the bugs that came out at night too and would hang around lights waiting to eat them. I think birds use to go after them which is probably why they were able to leave behind their tails, which incidentally re-grew.

Lynn McWilliam's family's car

The car above reminds me of my parents car which was a Triumph Herald. All the number plates started with SP (for Singapore), ours was SP 3040. We must have travelled miles in that car as we always seemed to be out and about.
I remember us being hemmed in traffic in Singapore. It felt like we were going to get crushed. Everyone just drove on any part of the road at the time. There must have been plenty of accidents.
When dad took the car to work, we'd catch the bus which was an experience in itself!

**Ellen Tait remembers: We bought a Triumph Herald car which was white with a red stripe, SP 3040, from Hong Heng's in Singapore. We kept it for the three years we were there.**
**Before that we hired a Toyota to go to Penang, it must have been one of their first models. Alan's knees almost touched the steering wheel and it had no petrol gauge. We never knew when we were going to run out!**

Brian Mitchell remembers:
Our family had never owned a car in the UK, not so unusual in the
1950s, and we lived in London where public transport was plentiful.
So I was pretty excited not just by going to Singapore but being told
we were going to be car owners when we got there! I guess the
normal practice for a Royal Air Force officer was to buy one second
hand from someone whose tour of duty had ended and sure enough
we were soon the proud owners of a rather old, but grand, Humber
Hawk, a huge tank of a car, leather seats and all.
This was okay but I pretty soon saw a number of my friends whose
families had large American cars, one family had a huge Nash (there
were about six kids) and across the road from our house sat another
US monster with huge fins. Our Humber Hawk looked pretty out of
date and tame in comparison.
We didn't have the Hawk long but worse was to come. Our next car
was a tiny grey little Standard. Our family of five hardly fitted into it
and not only did we travel around Singapore in it but we also
travelled across the Causeway to KL and a hill camp beyond
(incidentally this was not too long after the 'Emergency' and I still
recall the gates and fences, unused but still present, around villages
on the road up through Malaya).
Eventually before our return to the UK my father decided to get a
new car and ship it back to the UK, prices being much lower in
Singapore. So we began a tour of the car showrooms, including
visiting the Jaguar one for the unveiling of the 'E type' (in our
dreams were we going to end up with that one!) but at the first sight
of a Volvo, I knew my father had seen the car he wanted. It was duly
bought and arrived back at Liverpool docks in the UK some months
later.
Now, I guess, the Japanese cars dominate Singapore as so many
other places but I always associate my time there with those
wonderful old American gas guzzlers even if we never actually
owned one!

Kevin Daley remembers:
Here's a photo of my sister, Frances, at a Malayan birthday party.
This is the proof that most of our friends were local Malays and
Chinese.
I will always remember the fantastic meals their mothers cooked for
us. And the boys always wanted to borrow Mum and Dad's records
so that they could learn the music.

Ellen Tait remembers:
Alan would spend his pocket money on Satay sticks from a Malay
who made them on two biscuit tins filled with hot charcoal. He
carried them across his shoulders on a long pole!

Alan Cottrell's home at 27 Merryn Road in 1965. The television (we had one the same) and the furniture certainly brought back memories!

Alan Cooke's home at . 170 Rasah South, Serenban.

**John Harper remembers:**
**Acclimatisation was the process of getting used to the heat and the humidity. Arriving by ship had given us some time to get ourselves used to it. Nonetheless, we were told that it would be two weeks before we were allowed to go to school because we needed to**

acclimatize. Yippee!!

A friend of my father was on leave at that same time and took us to the beach nearly every day. This, of course, had to wait until my plaster cast was removed. I am pleased to say that my father had arranged that for the day after we arrived. What a relief to get rid of that awful encumbrance. That first experience of the sea, so warm, the sun burning down, the perfect balance of water temperature and air temperature, we felt that we had arrived in paradise. Despite the fact that Cleveleys is next to the sea, we had not learned to swim whilst living there. We were lucky if there were about half a dozen days per Summer when it was warm enough to go to the beach. We were taught to wade out in the water up to waist height and launch ourselves forward and to float in on an incoming wave. The water was so warm that you didn't stand about shivering on the water's edge wondering if you dare go in.

Soon, I was going deeper and was going to chest depth. Next thing I knew, I was having a go at breast stroke and managing to do that fairly well. Our swimming sessions were at the beach that ran alongside the runway at Changi. Moored out in the channel was a raft and before the two weeks acclimatization was up I could swim out to the raft without help. With the land reclamation that has gone on since, I think the beach area where I learned to swim has now become a part of the airport. I have joked with colleagues as we landed at Changi airport that I learned to swim on the perimeter track on the seaward side!

During those two weeks, we developed our tans, I think that was the real reason for the two weeks acclimatization as much as anything. Having blond hair also meant that our hair also lightened a few shades as well, the sun had a strong bleaching effect. During this period we met the local shop owner, Keng Wah Heng. His shop was just up the road from our house. We called in there and were treated to a cold drink. It seemed very strange to be served by a Chinese man wearing a sleeveless cotton vest. Heng's daughter, Chew, was of a similar age to us boys and often came to visit my mother whilst we lived at Lloyd Leas. Although my mother corresponded with Chew for some time when we returned to the UK, we lost touch during one of our moves. Also, during this acclimatization period, we were introduced to the Changi Bus company with a trip into the city. I think that in those days, the drivers only knew two accelerator positions, foot flat to the floor or foot off and onto the brake for a screeching halt. They used to hurtle along at an incredible pace and it was inadvisable to step out in front of one.

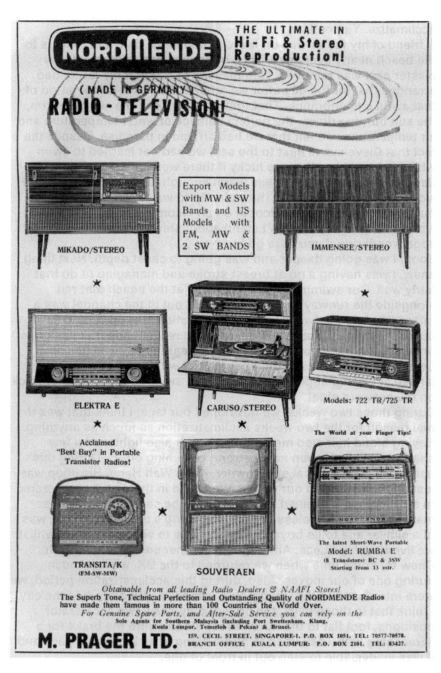

The modern appliances of the day that no home could do without!

**John Harper remembers:**
**After a few days, we started to explore Lloyd Leas estate on foot and I found that the Younger family, who had been quarantined on the boat, were living in the same road. So I ended up teaming up with Malcolm to further explore our surroundings. This took us down to Paradise Beach. This was a nice sandy cove with a sandstone cliff that had a house on top. Overlooking the cove was a pillbox that was said to have been built by the Japanese during World War Two, a fertile place for the imagination of young boys.**

Raymond Clayton with his mother and sister and his sister's friend Carol Strutt with John Harper in their front garden at Meteor Road, Tengah.

I suppose none of us will ever forget our homes in Singapore and Malaya. The all year round sunshine, apart from the monsoons, all the company from other forces' families and their kids, the wildlife, eating outside, the friendly people, the shopkeepers, short days at school and trips to allsorts of exciting places like Tiger Balm Gardens, the Zoo and Jason's Bay. I'll certainly never forget it and I'm sure that many of you reading this now would like to relive those days again. It's strange that many of our homes are still standing and inhabited by new families, most of who will probably never know all the fun that was once had there.

Five
# Around Singapore

Singapore, for me, was a smelly, hot, noisy place. I loved it though.
Especially all the toy shops and all the shops that just sold junk. I can
remember the smell of all the wicker work, the Wanchai Burberrys, the
meat from the local butcher's shop and, of course, the pong of the
Singapore River. Everywhere seemed busy with cars and taxis rushing
about, with men on bicycles, scooters and trishaws weaving in and out
between them. It may have been a lot quieter than I remember but, when
you're only a small boy, I'm sure it must have seemed very hectic.
I remember the Chinese bank and the free gifts that they had for children.
I got a money box in the shape of a safe which also played a tune when
you wound it up. There was always a man with one arm in the bank,
which has stayed in my memory since I was a kid.
Out on the streets were stalls selling everything you could want. There
were fruit sellers everywhere. I can still recall the smell of all that fruit
especially the rambutans and durians. The snake charmers and
magicians were fascinating to watch and they always drew a crowd.

A trishaw approaches the Thian Hock Seng Temple, 1960s. It was the
oldest Hokkien temple in Singapore. It was built in 1842 from funds raised
by rich Chinese merchants. Originally, there was a joss house on Telok
Ayer  Street where Chinese immigrants would meet. The Temple was built
to replace this. All the materials used to build it were brought from China.

My dad had visited Singapore with the Navy, before we went together as a family, and below are his recollections.

**Alan Tait remembers:**
**My first visit to Singapore was in September 1959. How long ago it seems! I was 23 years old and wide open to new experiences. I arrived there on board HMS Centaur which was an aircraft carrier. The ship was commissioned on the 3rd December 1958. She was 737 feet long with a beam of 128 feet. She carried 1,637 men which included the air squadrons. Between September 1958 and April 1960, she steamed 80,916 nautical miles and used 62,000 tons of fuel oil. Aircraft landed on her deck 7805 times. I promise no more statistics! The ship sailed through the Med. After the Suez Canal, our route took in Aden, Karachi, Cochin, Trincomalee and then Singapore. The ship had got hotter and more uncomfortable as we travelled further and further eastwards. When there was no flying taking place, everyone took the slightest opportunity to get on the flight deck.**

**The ship's movement caused a welcome breeze. Hours could be spent in the relative coolness watching all shapes and sizes of sea snakes and jellyfish drifting by. The many dolphins swimming effortlessly alongside and the flying fish skimming the surface were enthralling. Nevertheless, the heat on board was relentless, so when we were told we would be victualled in HMS Terror, during the docking period, it was a blessed relief!**
**The ship was taken into King George V dry dock. She was an impressive spectacle high and dry in the glorious sunshine.**

The accommodation at HMS Terror was on several levels with each level having lovely cool balconies.
We spent hours there writing letters home, chatting and playing cards etc. A short walk away was a swimming pool. Tiger Beer flowed like water. After life on board, this was just about paradise. Sembawang Village was close by with its duty free shops and bars. Cameras, watches, binoculars and all the usual was on offer at good prices. However, we were more fascinated with the toy shops. There were toys for sale that you couldn't find in the UK. We would have a good look at them all and soon the floor of the shop would be covered in toys, all battery operated including aeroplanes, robots, telephones and all sorts of gadgets. While we made our selections, we would be given a glass of Tiger Beer. The shopkeepers knew how to keep a customer happy. As with all of the local people, they were very polite, courteous and friendly. After a bit of bartering, our presents were wrapped up and ready for the kids back home.
Our visits to Singapore City itself were limited. We did have to work sometimes and our pay in those days was pretty poor. Nevertheless, Tiger Balm Gardens was a must to visit.

The gorilla statues near to the entrance of Tiger Balm Gardens.

The other attraction in town was the Britannia Club which was solely for service personnel. It had a magnificent swimming pool and restaurants and was situated across the road from the famous Raffles Hotel. We spent many a happy hour looking around the town and then relaxing in the club.

I recall taking a ride in a trishaw. A car clipped the side of it and we were dumped unceremoniously into the road as it tipped over. All the locals seemed to find it hilarious and it was just as well that nobody was hurt. The trishaw was a bit bent and, to rub salt into the wounds, the driver expected a tip!

The aircraft squadrons had flown ashore before we docked and spent time at RAF Seletar and RAF Butterworth. Any rest and relaxation they got was well earned as their working days were filled with danger. We lost several helicopters and planes during the commission and sadly, some of the pilots. A ship of this size was like a small village and any tragedy touched us all.

On the 3rd October, we spent a weekend at Pulau Tioman which is situated off the east coast of Malaysia.

It was my idea of a perfect tropical island with golden sands bleached by the sun and crystal clear blue water. It was completely uninhabited or so it seemed. We were landed by one of the ships' boats. The palm trees bent out towards the sea at such an angle that you could almost walk up the trunks. One of the sailors climbed up and started trying to knock down the coconuts. At this point, a native came out of the jungle and shouted,' Hey Jack! Leave my bloody coconuts alone!' He came from a tin hut which was just behind the tree line. All around the hut were the rotting husks of coconuts. He had an ample supply of coca-cola which he sold to anyone interested. I cannot imagine who he would sell to normally as we never saw another soul all of the time we were there. We had a wonderful day. I had flippers, mask and a spear gun. The waters were alive with fish of every colour and shape and the coral was spectacular. I caught several crayfish.

Back on board, at night, we bribed the chief chef with a tot of rum to cook them for us. They were delicious with a can or two of ice cold beer.

The ship sailed on from there to Hong Kong, Japan and all of the major ports of Australia.

We returned to Singapore in 1960 but not without mishap. We came alongside too quickly and crunched the dockyard wall and smashed a lamppost. The port anchor was huge and the shock of the impact shook it free. It landed on the jetty with a terrific thump.

I needed a haircut while we were in the harbour and there was a barber's shop in HMS Terror. I found out when I arrived that the barber was in fact a young Chinese girl. In those days, there were not any female barbers, so it was a bit of a shock. Nevertheless, I was soon in the chair with her clipping away in a competent manner. The next thing I knew, she was clipping away inside my ears and before I could stop her, the scissors were up my nose! I've had trims before but never one in so many places.

We left Singapore for the last time on the 4th February 1960 and finally arrived home in Plymouth on the 26th April 1960. We had been away for 3 days short of a year. I never dreamt that five years later I would return with my family and live there for three wonderful years.

Orchard Road as it was in the 1960s. It's changed quite a bit now and is more built up. Shops like Tangs have become larger departmental stores and there's a lot more traffic though it looks pretty busy in this scene too!

**Ellen Tait remembers:**
**We would sometimes get a taxi from JB to Singapore, it only cost a dollar, which was two shillings and four pence, in English money. It was very cheap and we travelled in a Mercedes. We'd go to Orchard Road and visit the cold store at Robinsons, just to cool down. Next, we'd visit The House Of Tang, an oriental Aladdin's Cave. It was full of camphor wood chests, carvings and all sorts of things you'd never see in England at the time. We still have a Bali wooden figure we bought there.**

**John Harper remembers:**
**First impressions of the city were of a multitude of smells and sights battering your senses. Exotic fruit, monsoon drains full of rotting detritus, Singapore River covered in junks from bank to bank, crazy taxi drivers, bicycle trishaws, food vendors cooking on clay pots, Chinese and Indian music, all these assaults on your senses came at you from every corner you turned. The gentile Western side of life was there as well with the department stores like Robinsons and eating places where you could get morning coffee and cream cakes. I must admit though that it was the exotic side that really made an impression on me.**

**Lisa White remembers:**
I will never forget the taste of Durian Ice Cream. I remember going to Penang and asking for a Vanilla Ice Cream and getting Durian instead. What a revolting taste and smell. I couldn't stand the smells of the markets but at the same time there was something nice about the smell of raw (rotting) fish and spices and vegetables in the Singapore heat or was that just me? I hated the red ants that lived in our sand pit and on the gate post where my brother always sat waiting for dad to come home. You'd think he would have learnt not to sit there after the first red ant attack! I hated dad always having to go away on flights but loved it when he came home and we would search every pocket in his flying suit looking for the goodies he always brought us back. I loved monsoon season and playing in the big monsoon drains but mum always put the fear of God into us warning us about hook-worm. I love (now) the innocence so many of us had living life in Singapore, being so lucky to be there (in 73-75) yet at the same time Vietnam was being destroyed. I wonder how I would have felt about it all if I was old enough to understand what my dad was doing on so many of those trips. Food for thought but I still feel very privileged to have experienced it and love my memories good and bad.

The route of the Magnolia Man.

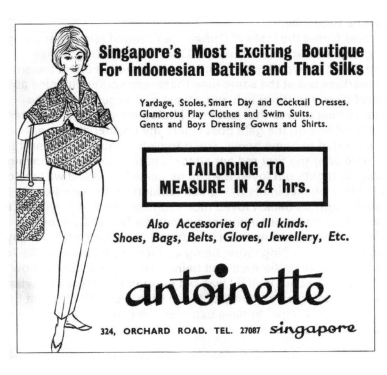

Antoinette, one of the many shops in Orchard Road catering for Westerners in the 1960s.

An advert for the NAAFI.

**Dee Hinton remembers the Magnolia Man:**
I remember Coke floats at the Cold Storage and the Magnolia ice cream man and his tricycle and the introduction of durian ice cream. Remember that smelly fruit? I also remember lychees, papayas ( I used to be a dab hand at climbing the tree in our garden to get them down) and mangosteens which stained our clothes.

**Leigh of the ANZ website remembers:**
Gosh, my likes: Satay from the satay man at Changi Air Force Base, the ice cream man, Maria's American Cafe in Changi (does it still exist?) weekends at the Family Club overlooking runway 2 of the Changi Air force base, roaming the jungles on Base, chasing Lee Kuan Yew's golf balls and selling them back to his guards for $1 a ball, discovering hidden Japanese pillar boxes, roaming the base without a care in the world, chasing the snakes from the garden, our Amah Sook Lim Moy (Susie) and her husband David (he drove a Changi Bus and always gave us free rides), taking one of the local ferries out to one of the islands and exploring the ruins and the surrounding countryside, eating at the hawker markets near Suicide Village, the weather, the shopping, Christmas dinner at the mess or at one of the hotels with their huge margarine sculptures of Santa with Asian eyes. My friends, and my school, being on milk duty and getting first choice out of the crates, the freedom we had to explore this strange and wonderful land and being able to proudly say years later, I grew up there and still think of it as home...

a **man's** taste starts with **Tiger**

Ask anybody who was in the forces at the time what drink they associated with Singapore and it would undoubtedly be Tiger Beer!

Bukit Timah Road 1963

**Tom O'Brien remembers:**
I used to live at the top of Hua Guan Avenue at No. 70. At the bottom of the Avenue was an estate, I think called Hock Sen Gardens, where there were a lot of RAF Servicemen and their families. The RAF men were mainly based at Tengah. There were some shops there and a cafe, which I used to go to for a coke or soft drink. I was told that these shops are now selling antique furniture etc.
I used to go to Beauty World a lot, often walking through the Kilburn Estate, crossing over the railway line and onto Bukit Timah. In those days, 1967, we had quite a bit of spending power as the exchange rate was just over $14 to the £1 although this was drastically cut in Nov 1967 when the Pound was devalued. I remember that there was so much happening around Beauty World itself, with all manner of stalls and hawkers. It was like an Ali Baba's cave, you could buy anything. I used to get my hair cut at an Indian barbers around the back of Beauty World. I remember his magazines were all written in Tamil, so all I could do was look at the pictures while I waited my turn. Facing Beauty World from the main road, on the right hand side, is where I used to exchange comic books and there was also a place where I used to get my shirts and trousers made. I used to get some outrageous brightly coloured shirts made up, bearing in mind that it was the hippy era and I was 14. We used to choose the

57

material and then have it made up.

The stall with the comic books was nearby. It sold second hand books. These were small A5 size comic war books. I think that 'Commando' might have been one of the titles. He had a huge selection and we'd spend ages looking through them all. Then if, say you bought 4, after you read them you'd take them back and exchange them 2 for 1. You usually ended up buying another couple as well. On the corner was a cafe. I remember that it was partitioned by a wall of drink crates full of empty bottles. I think he might have sub-let part of his premises. Quite often we would call in there for a coke or 7-Up. On my Mementoes page at Memories of Singapore, there is a receipt for a reel-to-reel tape recorder purchased at Beauty World. I remember badgering my mother for the $100 that it was going to cost. I'd never had a tape recorder before and so I asked if it could be my birthday present (15). I remember my Chinese friend Donald Foo telling me off because if I had asked him to get it, he could have purchased it a lot cheaper. I guess I couldn't wait to get this tape recorder. It lasted me a long time. I also remember my mother taking the family to the cinema in Bukit Timah to see 'The Jungle Book'. I can't remember where the cinema was or what it looked like.

Bukit Timah 7th mile in the 1960s. Beauty World was to the left.

**Ellen Tait remembers:**
We often used the Brit Club. We'd all meet up there and enjoy the facilities. It was opposite Raffles Hotel, famous for it's gin-slings and also for the famous people who went there. Not that we ever ate in there, it was too expensive! Only the famous could afford the prices! Instead, we would have a swim at the Brit Club and they served meals as well, what a lazy and enjoyable life it was!

**John Harper remembers:**
As well as the trip into the city there was also the trip into Changi village to be fitted up for school uniforms. Much time was spent selecting white cotton shirts, khaki shorts, white ankle socks and sandals. Then came the haggling over the price. 'I do special price for Missy because you buy so much'. I think my mother managed to get the price down by about another ten percent from his special price which, even by UK standards, was fairly cheap. This was a skill that she honed to a much better perfection during our stay.

Street scene at South Bridge Road in 1963. Hardly any cars and just one trishaw.

**Brian Mitchell remembers:**
We used to visit a record shop in Changi Village, not so much to buy records but to enjoy the air conditioning and to listen to the strange sounds they played. I think now it must have been modern jazz which at the time, I was completely unfamiliar with. I don't recall going to any music gigs other than seeing Cliff Richard and The Shadows play at a large indoor stadium somewhere in Singapore City, a big moment for both the Brits and local Singaporean fans of the day.

A policewoman directing the traffic.

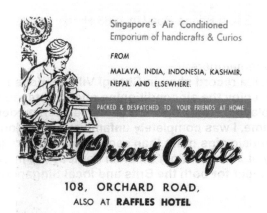
Many items in our parents' homes probably came from Orient Crafts on
Orchard Road.

Here, a trishaw moves along a street overflowing with food stalls and other wares.

**Brian Mitchell remembers:**
**We visited Tiger Balm Gardens, of course, and we had, what seems now, rather strange treasure hunts where families would get in their cars to follow a series of clues and drive all over the island in search of some 'treasure'. I can't imagine now why that was enjoyable! And there were also hill climbs, not on foot, but timed car races up a hill, maybe it was Bukit Timah Hill, I doubt in these environmentally aware days that this still goes on.**
**Perhaps the most popular outings of all for us kids from RAF Changi were the organised boat trips to beaches on Pulau Ubin, always an exciting time, away from the gaze of our parents!**

A Singapore dollar in the 1960s. It was worth about 2/6 then.

John Harper remembers:
By the end of the second week, I had realized that it was not a case of the Asians knowing my name was John, and that they all called English boys 'Johnny'. Up until then, I had wondered how they knew my name, although I never did like being called Johnny, it sounded so childish (even to a boy of ten). When I heard my brother Tom being called Johnny, 'clang', it dawned on me 'oh they call all English boys Johnny!'.

One of the many colourful lion dances.

Dee Hinton remembers:
I remember the race riots in 1964 when we had to leave the Naval Base by boat to land further around the coast and then be picked up to go on to Alex Grammar. I don't think I was at St John's then but can't remember the dates.
Also, I remember my father coming home with his uniform soaked in blood. Fortunately, it was someone else's! Mum and I often laugh at the fact that all the wives and children in our block of flats spent the evening together while the men were out dealing with the rioters. The wives armed themselves with carving knives and the children were issued with pots of pepper to throw in the eyes of anyone who may have broken in. For some totally inexplicable (or logical ) reason we camped out in one of the ground floor flats!
I remember sitting on an enormous crocodile that Dad had shot in the Senoko River. It had eaten a couple of locals so the police went hunting. It was brought back and laid out in the police station

which was down by Main Gate. Not sure what eventually happened to it but I seem to recall it was skinned to make bags or shoes etc. I remember playing in old air raid shelters, sledging down the hill from Bermuda Road towards Admiralty Road on sheets of corrugated iron and often finding snakes curled up under the sheets of iron when we lifted them.

Also, I recall sailing at Red House and watching the rain sweeping up the Straits of Johore towards us as we tried to make it back to Red House, particularly in the monsoon season. Other memories include the weekend regattas and the freshly squeezed lime juice made by the bar staff. Being wolf whistled by the sailors as we sailed past their ships. Oh, for the days when I could sail in nothing but a bikini! Chris Elsden and I had many a happy hour sailing and he and I are still in touch to reminisce.

Water skiing and falling off on the edge of a shoal of jelly fish. Ouch! I can still remember the pain! Watching the stingrays leaping out of the water as we skied and not taking too much notice of them. I wouldn't be so brave these days.

Trips up to Jasons Bay and Mersing. Flying foxes and bats. Haw Par Villa, the Van Cleefe Aquarium, shopping in Fitzpatricks and Tangs and feeding the cheeky monkeys in the Botanical Gardens. The endless rows of white crosses in the beautifully well looked after Kranji Cemetery.

Saturday morning cinema with one's little friends and then the back row of the cinema on Saturday nights as we got older!

Cycling everywhere until I got a scooter for my 16th birthday. The teenagers getting caught up in a night exercise after they broke into the electricity sub station by the swimming pool and turned off the Base lights. It became less of a joke when they were surrounded by blackened faces wielding guns and some got caught and arrested. Going to the docks to see people off and the streamers hanging off the ships' sides and the sirens hooting as they pulled away from the shore side.

Who can forget the smell of the Singapore River!

Going to cocktail parties with all those lovely Naval and Marine Officers and drinking Horses Necks and lethal G&T's. The Base being awash with sailors whenever ships berthed after an exercise and Naval Patrol being kept very busy.

Ros Wakeling and Peter Banks vanishing on a youth club outing and missing the transport home. They spent the night dodging the searchlights scanning the beach not realising it was a search party out looking for them, or so they said!

The Metropole Theatre, Maxwell Road.

The Metropole is now the Fairfield Methodist Church and is an official historical landmark in Singapore. Opposite is Maxwell Market. Many of the old cinemas and theatres in Singapore have now closed, some have become churches while others have become shopping centres. The Jubilee Theatre also disappeared when Raffles Hotel was expanded.

**Brian Mitchell remembers:**
**The cinema was popular, of course. For us 'Brit brats' with fathers based at the RAF Changi airbase we had outdoor films, few of which I recall except for some Elvis Presley films. My most vivid memory is of seeing 'Ben Hur' at a very large cinema in Singapore City. The film had its exciting moments but none more so than in the chariot race scene when the audience were all up on their feet cheering wildly! Much better than seeing the film in the UK where everyone just stays in their seat!**

**Gill Pennock remembers:**
**I loved eating out in Sembawang at the hawker stalls, satays from one, rice from another, sweet and sour from yet another. Hamburgers at the Cola Bar too.**
**Sundays all-you-could-eat at the Hyatt (and the magnificent ice sculptures they always had there). Buying the English comics at the**

little shop just inside the Admiralty gates every Saturday. Buying 45rpm records for $2 in Sembawang.

Mooncakes - have you tried them since? They just don't seem to taste the same as the ones the amah made. Rambutans, fresh pineapple, lychees.

Fresh lime juice outside the Kranji War Memorial and Walls ice creams from the man on the bicycle. The fish and chip van that came onto the base on Sunday nights.

My mum's driving licence photo. This is what the hairdressers of the day did to your hair if you sat still long enough!

The popular CK Tang store on Orchard Road.

The Capitol Theatre showing '36 Hours' starring James Garner and Eva Marie Saint. Coming soon was 'Girl Happy' starring Elvis Presley. The Shaw Building was very popular with cinema goers. Also showing at the time was 'The Secret Invasion' starring Stewart Granger and Mickey Rooney which would probably date this photo to 1965.

The Thieves Market 1963.

**John Cunningham remembers:**
Interestingly, just to the left of the old Raffles Square, was a small alley called Change Alley (on its corner was the Magnolia Ice Cream parlour). It ran down to Collyer Quay if I remember and it's there in Change Alley a collection of small traders sold everything from cameras to TVs to umbrellas (they'd actually give you a brolly if it was raining and you couldn't agree a price!) to tools.
It was tools we were after at the time, to supplement our RAF ones or to get them as personal kit for our motorbikes.
I remember I spotted a set of Chrome Vanadium 'drop forged' spanners and started to haggle over the price, when the trader kept dropping them on the concrete floor. 'See', he cried, 'dlop forged, dlop forged!'. Trouble was that he'd dropped them so often one of the set was actually bent! Mind you what could you expect for 3 dollars (a dollar at that time was about 22p).
Great laugh indeed but I have to confess that you could get some amazingly good stuff from there and it was a real shopping haunt for servicemen, as was Bugis Street, but that is another story entirely!
Still on shopping, we also were short of a piece of aircraft kit called 'Blue Parrot' ,a real techy sort of experimental radar gear and whilst in 'Thieves Market', as it was called, blow me we found a complete set of the stuff! Don't even ask where or how, anyway we haggled a

price and took it back .The stores quartermaster simply could not believe it! And it worked!
Of course it wasn't called Thieves Market for nothing, was it? (Ferranti 'Blue Parrot' was an airborne radar designed to detect Russian cruisers and barely in service with us at the time! ).

Change Alley 1960s.

**Ellen Tait remembers: Change Alley in Singapore was a great place for bargains. You could barter all day and still get seen off! It was still cheaper than at home and that was all part of the fun. The Amah's Markets were great as well. We use to go to one up the Bukit Timah Road, they were very colourful at night and the lights attracted huge moths. I bought two round green chairs there for the equivalent of 5 shillings each at English prices. We brought them home and  we had them for years, they lasted well.**

Change Alley was a great place to barter and you always ended up with a bargain. The shopkeepers would do anything to get you into their shops and once you were in, they nearly always managed to sell you something or other. Every time you would walk away, the price would get lower until it was so low, you bought whatever it was anyway. Probably most people didn't want the stuff in the first place though it was a great place to buy watches, cameras and electrical goods.

Ellen Daley at Change Alley 1960s.

A later shot of Change Alley, during a quieter period.

A more busy scene at Change Alley in 1970.

A shopkeeper in Sembawang 1970, selling paintings and jewellery.

**Dee Hinton remembers shopping in Sembawang:**
**Kutty's Garage, Shell petrol and where we picked up a taxi ( usually a Merc), Wah Hin's ( the grocery store who delivered) and Ismael's (the newsagents). We used to go and order our annuals for Christmas from them. All these were down by Sembawang Gate on the inside. Outside were the bars, Toothy Wong (the tailor who knocked up a suit in hours), Mr Lee the photographer ( I should think everyone must have at least one picture taken by him as he covered all the functions), the dress shop where you took in a picture in a magazine and some fabric bought off a market stall and they produced a perfect fitting dress. The shoe shop that drew around your feet and produced wonderfully comfortable shoes and Ahamedsa who gave everyone in the family generous presents at Christmas to thank them for being such good customers (John Lewis take note!).**

The Adelphi Hotel.

The Adelphi Hotel was on Coleman Street and was one of the principle hotels in Singapore at the time along with Raffles Hotel, Hotel de L'Europe and Hotel de La Paix. The Hotel closed on the 25th June 1973 and it was demolished in 1980. The Adelphi complex now stands in its place.

An advert for Raffles Hotel 'Renowned to Travellers the World Over'.
The Raffles Hotel will be remembered fondly by service men and their
families. I'm not sure we ever went in it though - it was probably too
expensive!

North Bridge Road at night.

**Brian Mitchell remembers:**
In the 1960s, Upper Changi Road was the main route between Changi Village and the city and buses flew down it every few minutes at busy times. And what buses they were! They were old and well used, rattled like mad and travelled with all the windows down and that was just as well because they had shaken and rattled so much that the window glass had gone crazed and was opaque, nothing could be seen through them! Those buses were the main means of transport for me and my friends , no Mass Transit System existed in those days. We would wait on Upper Changi Road for our frequent trips to the Village and the airbase swimming pool. Suddenly, a bus would fly over the brow of the hill near Changi prison and it might be more than one, they seemed to race each other and sometimes arrived in groups. Then we would rush onto the hard seats and spend the journey sliding around and hanging on as the bus flew onwards. There are two other things I always recall about those buses, if you travelled at night you might see the biggest cockroaches ever. And then there were the bus tickets. Well, the tickets need explaining. They were small coloured card tickets and they had numbers on them. Being teenage boys, we had a game with those numbers. Add up the digits and if they came to a special number, like 18 or 21, then you were in luck with your girlfriend - I won't go into more detail! I wonder if similar games go on today? So, I wonder what the buses are like today? Air-conditioned and cockroach free? Driven carefully, with comfortable seats and with no rattles?

The buses were certainly different in Singapore at the time. Breakdowns were common and sometimes everyone would get off the bus and give it a push. If it wouldn't go, everyone got off and waited until the next one! There were no queues and everyone would just pile on. My dad's friend Omar at KD Malaya came to England once and assumed that everyone just piled onto the buses here too. So, when the bus came, he just went to the front of the queue. A big matelot grabbed him by the shoulders and put him to the back of the line, I don't think he ever did it again. The buses in Singapore not only struggled to go but were also overcrowded. I remember people bringing live chickens home from the market for that night's tea and they would be running everywhere. There were also huge fish wrapped in newspaper. Sometimes these items would be forgotten about and left on the bus. If it happened to rain, the windows would all leak so people would move away from the outer seats. Of course, there was a smell to the bus of food, fish and chickens but strange smells were no surprise in Singapore at the time!

A typical Chinese street with fruit stalls overflowing onto the road.

# THE HOUSE OF TANG

*A range of Oriental Gifts to delight your heart*

CURIOS, IVORY, JADE
EMBROIDERED LINEN
CARVED, TEAKWOOD FURNITURE & CHESTS,
BATIK, CROCODILE SKIN BAGS
CAMERAS, RADIOS & PERFUMES

## C. K. TANG [SINGAPORE] LTD.

310, Orchard Road, Singapore, 9. Tel. 34025

The House of Tang. Everything you needed, and some things you never needed, all under one roof! A visit to Tangs was great. There probably wasn't a serviceman's home in Singapore and Malaya that didn't have something bought from there.

A stall holder selling magazines, newspapers and other trinkets in the
heart of Singapore.

A dragon dance taking place in the evening.

**Kevin Daley remembers: Okay, if you had never seen a dragon before it could be scary. But the drums beating and music was nothing compared to the fire crackers when they went off!**

Anderson Bridge in the heart of Singapore.

The Sri Mariamman Temple in South Bridge Road in Chinatown. It's the oldest Hindu temple in Singapore. I'm sure it must appear in thousands of photos taken during the 1960s. It was highly decorated with Hindu Gods and colourfully painted statues.

The many sampans inhabiting Singapore River in the 1960s. The river was once full of boats but now, since it's been cleaned up, it's quite empty.

**Clive Baker remembers:**
The Brit Club was home from home for Singapore based service personnel. Here you could get egg, bacon and chips with Daddies sauce, a couple of slices of real bread and real PG Tips type tea. Of course, there was also the fact that it sold really cheap Tiger beer and it was here that I was first introduced to what was to become a life-long habit, I still enjoy the occasional pint of Tiger Tops and it certainly is a good reason for going back to Singapore for the real McCoy, straight from the tap instead of a bottle!

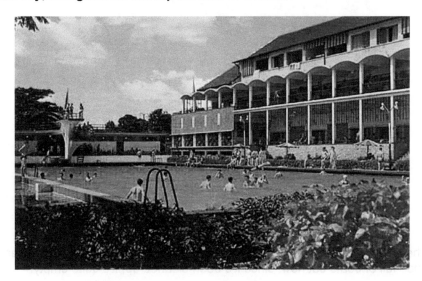

The Brit Club.

Ron Spurrier at the Nuffield Pool in the Brit Club.

The Nuffield Pool with Ron Spurrier on the right.

John Harper remembers:

School was from 8.00am each morning until 12.30pm each day and, to make up the hours, included Saturday mornings. So leisure time was all afternoon and evening plus Sundays. For many of us kids, it was get the homework done and then head straight down to the swimming pool. These were particularly good pools going from about 2 feet 6 inches deep to 11 feet at the deep end with a springboard, ten foot board and twenty foot board. We would be in and out the water and there was always a session at the NAAFI kiosk - Coke or Pepsi and coconut ice. At the end of the afternoon, it would be onto our bicycles and pedal back across the runway and back home for tea. Round about six in the evening, it would get dark and that would be the signal to head for home, listen to Radio Malaya and then about eight in the evening, it was off to bed ready to get up early for the next morning. Next morning about 6:00am, it was time to get up to head down to the city for another day at school.

Once a week there was a Scouts meeting and that was one of the few days that we were ever allowed to stay up late when there was school the next day. We had some amazing times. My first experience of camping was when we went off to the Singapore Scouts campsite at Jurong. At the gate into the camp, we collected tents, pots and pans and duckboards for sleeping on. We wondered what these were for. The camp site was on bare clay and we erected the tents finding it difficult to knock the pegs in. There was also advice that we should dig a trench around the tent but the ground was baked so hard that we managed to chip only about an inch channel. Two days later, when it rained, the lesson of keeping everything off the ground and the need for a channel round the tent was quickly learned. With a typical tropical thunderstorm, the minuscule trench quickly filled with water and within five minutes the tent was like a streambed. We quickly put on swimming trunks and went out in the rain with spades and dug the trench about six inches deep piling the soil between the trench and the tent to improve the barrier. Digging was, of course, much easier now that the clay was wet. The following day we rolled the sides of the tent up to allow all of the wet bedding and clothing to dry. Typically, having dug the trenches, there was no more rain all the time that we were there.

The site was plumbed with toilets and showers albeit cold showers but they were quite refreshing in the Singapore heat. Next to the site was a rubber plantation and each morning the tappers would come round to collect the accumulated latex and cut a new slice of channel to keep the latex flowing.

In the scout troop there were several Asian boys from the Tengah village just next to the RAF Tengah base. There was Kim who was Chinese, Johari an Indian Muslim and Ranjit who was Indian Sikh. There were one or two others but my memory lets me down and I can't remember their names. Mixing with Asians at this young age and having a Canadian mother taught me the value of racial tolerance. I feel that it greatly enriched me although I didn't realise it at the time. We all mucked in together with general tasks, games and learning together.

One of the highlights of the camping trip was a visit to the old Japanese submarine pens where we all went fishing. It was rumoured that there was an octopus in the pens and there was even a tale that a boy from the RAF Changi troop had slipped in the water and came out with octopus tentacles wrapped around his leg. It sounds a bit far fetched to me now but when I was eleven it sounded fairly plausible! On the way back to the campsite, Mike the scoutmaster bought a load of pineapples for our lunch the following day. Each patrol was given some custard powder to make custard to go with the fruit. One lad said that he knew how to make custard and proceeded to make it whilst the rest of us got on and trimmed up the pineapples and created pineapple rings. Everybody lined up and was given their allocation of two pineapple rings and then the custard was poured on. We all sat down and before too long there was much groaning and moaning when we tasted the custard. Our custard expert had only forgotten to put the sugar in. Anyway, once the custard was scraped off, the pineapple rings were wonderful, there was nothing to compare with the taste!

We had a few trips with the Scouts and one that was really good fun was a trip to Pulau Ubin, a small island just off the coast from Changi. We travelled over from Tengah and then caught a motorised canoe over to the small island where we bivouacked under army capes and cooked food over open fires. In those days, the island had very few inhabitants and the main activity was quarrying. Much of the timber work in the quarry had been lashed together using square and diagonal lashings. The spot we camped on was directly under the flight path for aircraft coming in to land at Paya Lebar airport which was the main Singapore airport in those days. I can remember seeing Constellations with the triple tail and Brittanias.

Aside from swimming and scouts, a gang of us would often gather on our bikes and go off to the scrubland at the end of road and meet in one of the perimeter fence towers. There we would usually gather some wood and make a fire and smoke the cigarettes we had pinched from our parents. It was all bravado stuff, I don't think anybody ever inhaled the smoke. There was also a little bit of woodland with a few remains from a crashed Beaufighter nearby and we often used to gather round it and drift off into fantasies of being a pilot and shooting down Japanese warplanes. One time when we visited the wreckage, I found a papery snake skin that had been shed. A few weeks later, I was confined to home with a really bad cold. The group had met at the wreckage without me and my friend John Smith, and yes that was his real name, picked up what he thought was a shed snake skin. It turned out to be a sleeping cobra! Fortunately, before it could bite him, he was quick-witted enough to throw it away from himself and the snake slithered off into the undergrowth. Another gathering place was the old disused Japanese runway. Being boys, there had to be a gruesome tale attached to the runway and there may be an element of truth in it. The tale was that the runway was built by prisoners of war, many of who were slaughtered on the spot and thrown into the diggings to be covered over with foundation material. Out of respect for the dead prisoners, when the Japanese surrendered the runway was decommissioned and allowed to fall into disrepair.

Because we spent so much time at the swimming pool our hair turned dramatically lighter and picked up a green tinge. I'm not sure whether it was colouration caused by the chlorine in the water or whether it was being coloured by minute algae.

Whilst we lived at Lloyd Leas, one of my favourite pastimes was to go down to Paradise Beach for a swim and inspect the machine gun pill box that stood guard over the cove. I remember one day going down there and there was a very high tide so we laid on top of the sea wall and watched the small fish feeding around the wall. Suddenly, the sky turned black and there was a whizzing noise. When we looked up, there was a whirlwind waterspout right in front of us. My mother shepherded us straight into the pill box where we watched it traverse the cove, coming about two feet in front of the pillbox, and then make its way out to sea and fizzle out. It was an incredible sight.

Sunday afternoons were always quiet and I would sometimes save a few prawns from my Nasi Goreng that I always had at the families club for Sunday lunch. I would then head down to the fenced in swimming area next to Changi Yacht Club known as the Pagar and spend the afternoon fishing, using the prawns I had saved as bait. Sunday afternoons in Changi village would often see large groups of people playing Mah Jong and cards. The atmosphere in the village was always very relaxed on Sunday afternoons.

Penang Road.

**Jo-Anne Rendle and the children of NZ Services School Woodlands Primary 1976, remember some of the things they liked, at the time, about Singapore:**

**Eating satay off sticks after dipping them into the tasty hot sauce that goes with them, seeing the rubber plantations with the rubber trees all leaning in the same direction, my amah, our guard dog and all the chitchats that came out at night to eat insects, watching the Chinese New Year Parade with all the decorated floats and the people in their lovely, bright colourful costumes, going to children's days at the Metro department shops, seeing all the birds at the Jurong Bird Park, especially the beautiful peacocks, eating all the local fruits like mangoes, rambutans, pineapples and papaya, having ham sandwiches often because ham is cheaper in Singapore than at home, the Sergeants mess, having rides on trishaws and seeing the indian temples, our grocer because he is much cheaper than our grocer at home, watching the snake charmers and their snakes, having fans and air conditioning to keep us cooler on hot days, all our friends and teachers and the art we use to do at school, seeing the actors in the Wayangs or Chinese Operas with their heavy make-up and fancy, bright costumes, looking at the big ships in the Naval Basin, the articulated Se Land trucks and the local trucks that didn't have any doors, the smell of frangipani and the fresh, warm smell after a heavy, tropical downpour.**

Duncan Gordon remembers eating out in Singapore:
The stall was well lit and under the light, every detail could be seen, including the two broken bricks a table was jacked up on. The jagged, knocked, scratched yet clean linoleum table tops, the low lying canvas over our heads, green and mildewed and the cracked uneven concrete under our feet.

Over in one corner you could see a middle aged Chinese man dressed in a pair of shorts and a tee-shirt with two Chinese women dressed in their national costume, working over a gas fire preparing meals with a huge knife and taking orders.

Around the fire were a few tables, a cupboard and the oldest fridge you ever did see, packed so full its glass doors could hardly close. We decided to order some bean shoots, fried rice, chicken 'a la king' and fu yung hai. The dishes were put in the middle of the table and we were given a small round bowl each and wooden slender chopsticks.

Eating with chopsticks for the first time is an awkward, embarrassing but amazing experience and the meal would not have been complete if we had not been in typical Chinese surroundings.

Rickshaws waiting for customers in downtown Singapore.

The Sultan Mosque in Arab Street. The gold dome of the mosque was a landmark and visible from many parts of Singapore. The shops on the right have now gone to reveal more of the original building. Arab Street features many shops selling food, goods and brightly coloured textiles.

Jo-Anne Rendle and the children of NZ Services School Woodlands Primary 1975 remember some of the things they disliked, at the time, about Singapore:

Singapore milk tasted awful, it was good to have New Zealand milk when we returned home, being frightened by cockroaches when they rushed toward us after being disturbed from their hiding places in dark cupboards, the sunburn on our faces. being stuck in a traffic jam on a hot day, hearing the thunder and lightning when there was a bad thunderstorm close by, seeing snakes, even if they were non-poisonous, the thought of having to start at another school when we went back to New Zealand, the air pollution and the strange smells of the rubber factories and village markets, fish from the market because our amah bought some and they were rotten, not having any of our relations living close enough to visit, Singapore beer, you can get D.B back in New Zealand, people who spit on the ground where you walk, not having four seasons each year and being unable to snuggle under the blankets during cold nights in winter, not being able to buy short pyjama pants. the sound of frogs and toads croaking in the monsoon drains after it has been raining, being bitten by ants every time you sat on the ground. having to sleep under a mosquito net at night. leaving our pets behind when we went back to New Zealand, seeing traffic accidents and saying good-bye to friends.

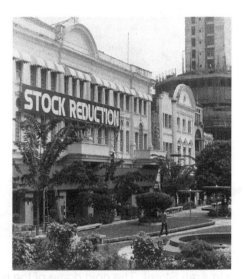

Robinsons department store.

The Cathay Hotel was opened in 1939 and included a 1,300 seat cinema which we probably all visited in the 1960s. The Hotel ceased trading in the 1950s and became apartments. The cinema was Singapore's first air conditioned cinema and you could sit in an armchair to watch the films. The Cathay was redeveloped and reopened with a new cinema complex in 2006. Part of it was listed as a National Monument and many of the old features were kept.

Chinatown was mainly populated by Chinese and was in the larger district of Outram. Chinatown was largely overpopulated in the 1960s until the government relocated many of the people to new housing areas. Chinatown includes Pagoda Street, Smith Street, Temple Street, Trengganu Street and New Bridge Road. It's famous for the letter writers of Sago Street, its sandalwood idols at Club Street and the food at Mosque Street.
In these two pictures can be seen washing hanging out of windows on poles and the many stalls that inhabited the streets. It was a great place to visit and to get a taste of the Chinese way of life.

Another shot of Chinatown. The man is shorts looks like the genie
from Aladdin!

Sembawang Village 1960s.

Sembawang was home to the Woodlands Naval Base. Some of us went to school there and many of our fathers worked inside. The area has now changed greatly. There is more modern housing built there now and even a Sembawang MRT station.

The photo above reminds me of what the area looked like around our home at Jalan Wijaya in Malaya in the 1960s. Apparently, it's hard to recognise most of Sembawang nowadays!

Sembawang Village.

Local children, Sembawang, 1970.

Lakki Bar and Restaurant, Sembawang.

Sembawang village. There is a Triumph Herald on the right which was very similar to our family car then.

A kampong at Bukit Timah just behind the City Lights Bar, 1960. It's amazing that these Kampong's stood so near to the main city and its more modern buildings.

Another kampong tucked away in Singapore, 1960.

A street bookseller selling by lamplight, 1970.

**Kevin Daley remembers:**
**I think one of my favourite foods was chicken satay sticks. Mouth watering. Nasi Goreng was also quite popular and I even tried shark's fin and birds nest soup. Had I known a bit more about how they are made and the effect on the relevant animals, I doubt they would have been high on my list.**
**Back on the 'slaughter of animals' theme (not for the squeamish). Did you ever go into the JB market where they prepared the chickens? Ray and I went down there one day and saw all these chickens packed into small baskets. We ventured into a building and saw people reaching into the baskets to pull a chicken out by the neck. With a swift flick of the wrist they bent the neck back and applied a quick slit on its throat. The chicken was then pulled down onto a hook that was suspended from a long conveyor that snaked its way around the building. There was an endless number of chickens flapping about from the conveyor. The next stage saw the chickens pass into an inner building, the bulk still alive. At the exit point it was obvious that they had been subjected to steam and high temperatures. Most chickens had little or no feathers left on them.**

Food stall, Sembawang, 1970.
You can almost smell and taste all the cooked food here.

**John Harper remembers:**
**Singapore food was, and still is, famed for its variety, quality and taste. You can find every taste of the globe in Singapore. It was a family ritual to go to the families club overlooking Changi airfield every Sunday for lunch. For the first few weeks, as my brothers and I were fairly young and unadventurous with food, it was egg and chips with lashings of tomato sauce. Each week, our parents would try to persuade us to try something from the Asian food part of the menu. Each week, we steadfastly refused and ordered egg and chips. I was the first to give in and was persuaded to try the special fried rice. There was ham, chicken and prawns in it. After the first mouthful, I thought, 'wow, why have I been so silly and been insisting on egg and chips all these weeks?'. I would like to say that I branched out into all sorts of dishes, but no, fried rice was safe and I stuck with that for some time. Eventually, I did get more adventurous and started to work my way down the menu.**
**Once a week, one of the restaurants in Changi Village made curry puffs, a parcel of curried minced meat in puff pastry. Curry was something that we had experienced back home in the UK, you know, the fairly mild stuff with apple and raisins in it. We quickly adapted to the stronger taste and heat of real curry and the curry puffs were a**

regular favourite. After a few months in Singapore, my father instituted a family tradition of going into the city on the first Sunday of each month. It was always fairly predictable, taxi in to the Union Jack club and we boys would spend a couple of hours in the swimming pool being fed Cocoa Cola when we got thirsty. Dad, of course, would be slaking his thirst with Tiger or Anchor beer. After the pool, we would then go to the Islamic restaurant on Beach Road. It was here that we were introduced to Indian curry. I have to admit I was a bit worried at the thought of possibly a very hot curry and went into defensive mode. 'Do they have fried rice?' I asked. 'Well sort of!' my father replied, 'but it's a little bit different to Chinese fried rice and it is called Briyani!'. A little fearfully, I said, 'Okay, I'll have a prawn Briyani!' Brother Tom followed suit and after a bit of humming and hawing, Bob agreed to try it as well.

The food arrived and 'Wow!'. Mum and Dad had ordered chicken curry of some sort and we were given side dishes of boiled egg, mango pickle, pineapple, peanuts and shreds of coconut. The three dishes of Briyani arrived with their dishes of curry sauce. The table was groaning under the weight of it all. The taste was absolutely out of this world. I had never tasted anything like it before in my life. The combination of spices, the fresh prawns and the flavoursome rice was the epitome of perfection. Instant conversion, even to this day, Prawn Briyani is one of my favourite dishes. I'm drooling at the thought of it even now almost fifty years later.

Curry now became a regular part of our diet. My mother even sent a recipe back to her friend in the UK who had originally given her the recipe for curry with raisins and apple in it. She included several side notes in it like, 'Yes, that really is dessert spoons and not teaspoons!', and a warning, 'You'll find that it has a very warming sensation!'.

Food seemed to be an integral part of being in Singapore. In fact one thing that you were often asked is not, 'How are you?' but 'Have you eaten yet?' As you walked along the five foot way, you would often come across somebody sat with a clay pot charcoal barbecue, cooking sticks of Satay. Satay is another of the wonderful dishes of Asia. Meat is marinated in a spicy sauce with chillies, ginger, lemon grass to name but a few of the ingredients and served with a spicy sauce containing coarsely ground roast peanut. As darkness fell, Changi Village would come alive with hawker stalls. Often the self-contained stall was built around a tricycle making it extremely mobile. They would be lit with a paraffin fuelled Tilley lamp. The most popular dish seemed to be noodles, which of course came in all sorts of shapes and sizes.

Food arriving on bicycle wheels seemed to be a normal part of everyday life. The Magnolia ice cream man would arrive, park his bike on the stand, one of those pull-down jobs on the back wheel that lifted the back wheel off the ground. The ice cream was in an insulated box mounted on the carrier over the back wheel. He would ring his hand bell as soon as he had parked his bike and be surrounded by mothers and children seeking to purchase his wares. Inside the insulated box must have been like a timelord's Tardis because there were family sized blocks, wafer blocks in a variety of favours, and ice lollies, milky strawberry or plain milky, blackcurrant, strawberry and even Durian ice lollies.

Durian is a fruit that I can only describe as an acquired taste that I never managed to acquire, just as I have never acquired a taste for some of the riper cheeses. To me the smell of the fruit was like an open sewer. Even on returning to the east several times over the intervening years, I find that I just cannot get my nose past that smell despite trying several times. It has been described as having the smell of a drain but a taste like heaven. It is a highly prized fruit for Asians and it is a great compliment to be offered a slice. I found that I had to mentally close my nostrils and try to keep them closed whilst I ate the fruit. It never really worked and it is probably the only fruit that I have never taken to, despite my best efforts. My brother Bob, however, quite liked durian. His work often took him to Asia, (lucky man), and he used to tell the tale of how he once bought a couple of durians and walked through Robinsons department store. By the time he left the store, there were six female sales assistants following him and the aroma of his durians.

Fruit, of course, was another food that arrived on bicycle wheels. The fruit seller was known as Mary and she had an amazing variety of fruit for sale. There were pineapples, apples and oranges, mangosteens and my particular favourite, rambutan. The rambutan is related to the Lychee but the skin has long hairy like protrusions that give it its name, as rambut is Malay for hair. This might sound a little off-putting but the red skin peels away easily just as if you were peeling a thick skinned orange and then inside you find what looks a little bit like a white plum. The white fruit covers a stone. Biting into the fruit, it is juicy, fragrant and sweet without being excessively sour. Describing the fragrance is difficult and all I can say is that it is rambutan. If pressed, I would describe it as floral, sweet maybe a hint of lavender, maybe a hint of orange but only the vaguest hint as the fragrance is so subtle. This might all sound a bit pretentious or even a bit wine buff, but I can only say, that's rambutans and I love them and I would gladly pay the air fare to go back and taste them again and again if only I could afford it.

Having mentioned Mary I must digress from the topic of food and in doing so I make no apologies as I am raising a very interesting and important point. Mary was an extremely exceptional lady, not only did she give rambutans to the children who patronised her stall, which in my book made her pretty special, she had also been awarded the OBE. She was really a special lady, as some of the prisoners of war in Changi Prison will testify. She played an important part in helping escaped prisoners and it was for this that she was awarded the OBE. On the return to British rule, she was granted the freedom to sell her fruit anywhere on the military bases at Changi. I know this is only a short paragraph but Mary probably merits a whole book to herself and I hope that somebody will do the research one day on a topic that will reward the researcher tenfold. So having made that important digression from the subject of food let us return to the topic in hand. I was going to say that one of the strangest fruit was the Pomello but there are probably other candidates with equal provenance to the claim. Anyway, the Pomello was a fruit we tried and it was a citrus fruit about the size of a melon that was like a cross between a grapefruit, but not as bitter, and a fragrance with a hint of orange. The flesh inside was segmented in a typical citrus fashion but inside the segments the soft bead like structure of an orange or lemon was a bit more fibrous and you could remove little sachets of fruity, juicy material and pop them in your mouth one by one.

I mentioned Mangosteens earlier, the skin is semi-hard and purple and likely to stain whatever it comes into contact with. The flesh inside, once again, is juicy and distinctive, impossible to liken to anything from Europe. All I can say is, travel to the Far East and try it for yourself.

To correct any impression you might have that life was one exotic eating orgy (maybe it was), the amah used to prepare what we considered as perfectly normal English dishes. Her repertoire included egg and chips, mince and mash, pork chops with peas and mash as well as the exotic dishes like curry. Sunday roasts were very rare though, as it was the amah's day off and we usually went to the families club for lunch (special fried rice).

Singapore changed my outlook on food. Rice was no longer a dish that was served as a sweet pudding. Rice had a thousand and one possibilities, it also came in many varieties although, at this time, I was only able to differentiate two types, short grain for rice puddings and long grain for savoury dishes. Nowadays I prefer boiled rice to boiled potatoes but I do have to admit that any form of fried potato is almost equal to any form of rice, boiled, fried or risotto. The one exception to this would be "congee" or rice porridge. It's a nice non-irritant dish when you have diarrhoea but it has nothing else much to commend it although the Tanjong Pagar area of Singapore is noted for it where it is served with all sorts of extras (it needs it).

It was almost impossible to avoid soggy breakfast cereals with the high humidity and we very quickly adapted to the Australian version of Weetabix called Weet Bix. The biscuit was a lot harder and seemed very resistant to humidity problems. Fresh milk was virtually unheard of and so powdered milk (KLIM) was the norm. We had a special mixer for making up the milk. A tall glass cylinder was three quarter filled with water from the refrigerator, powdered milk added and then a plunger with perforations in the disc introduced into the cylinder to push the powdered milk up and down to get it wet and dissolve. It required several minutes of vigorous pumping to get all the powder to dissolve.

As well as the all time favourites Coca Cola and Pepsi Cola a whole range of soft drinks were available at the NAAFI and swimming pool including Ice Cream Soda, Sarsaparilla, Lemonade, Orangeade, Cherryade and Ginger Beer. Ice cream soda was nice with a scoop of ice cream in it and was known as an Ice Cream Soda float. Other favourites at the pool were the Coconut Ice slabs and my good friend Raymond Clayton reminded me recently that you could also get giant pickled onions at the pool. I met up with Raymond 40 years after we had been in Singapore after bumping into his elder brother at a Singapore schools reunion that was held in London. The reunion was also a chance to relive the food as the group usually goes on to Soho for a Chinese meal afterwards.

I'm also pleased to say that I still enjoy food in Singapore whenever I have made visits related to my work. I am a fan of the food courts and hawker stalls. Early childhood influences have certainly left their mark on my food preferences.

Kevin Daley remembers:
Sembawang fishing ponds. At last, we convinced mum and dad to take us here. Unfortunately, the Chinese boy next to me kept catching MY fish. I couldn't believe my eyes when he reeled in and all he had on the end of his line were a bunch of treble hooks and no bait. He was content to foul-hook everything.

My brother Ray and I had started to fish whilst we lived in Rosyth, Scotland. We felt you couldn't beat throwing a hook into the murky cold waters of the Firth of Forth. To sit there for hours on end waiting and hoping for the big one was heaven! In fact, our claim to fame was fishing from the middle of the Forth Road Bridge whilst it was still under construction! Playing cat and mouse with the security guards on their mopeds always added to the excitement. However, the warm and clear waters of the rivers, lakes and sea around JB and Singapore proved an overwhelming draw to two young boys. We had set our sites on these amazing rods and reels we had seen in shops in JB and it was not long before we were the owners of Diawa fishing gear! We had arrived.

On most fishing trips, we headed down to the pier at JB, along the Skudai or from the western side of the causeway, to fish. More often than not, we would be fishing next to local children who were more than impressed with our Diawa tackle. The majority of locals fished with a long piece of bamboo or sugar cane (very similar to the long poles you see people fishing with today), with a line tied to the end. It wasn't long before we got caught up in the competition to see who could catch the most fish in the shortest period of time. The water used to be crystal clear and you were able to place your baited hook

100

directly in front of the fish you wanted to catch. Guess what? With all the new technology available to both Ray and I, we never once won this contest. The time it takes to wind in, renew the bait, cast and draw into position proved too excessive. In the blink of an eye, our competition were catching fish after fish. Another lesson learnt. It wasn't the end of our Diawa gear but we both learnt that to give the locals a fair match, we had to play on the same field.

Once we got back home, we drew up new battle plans which we would put into action on our next fishing trip. Within days we were off again. The Daiwa tackle remained at home.

Action 1 was to move away from our worm and prawn baits and acquire the same bait that the local children seemed to have great success with and all it needed was a visit to the bakery that was close to JB pier. Having handed over a few cents, we left with the *killer bait.* We had bought a large lump of warm dough!

Action 2 saw us enter the market area alongside the Sweet Water Canal. Here we were able to buy long lengths of bamboo for a few cents.

Within minutes we were back on the pier and equalling the strike record of our local fishing colleagues.

Ray and I returned to the bus station for the ride home feeling pretty pleased with the outcome. We had held our own against the skill and expertise of the local children and had barely dipped into our pocket money. However, it was the bus driver that soon wiped the smile of our faces. He refused to let us onto the bus with lengths of bamboo that must have been around 15 feet long. He made us break off around 3 or 4 feet from the tip before we could carry it onto the bus. I felt this was a bit harsh and guessed we must have been fishing against one of his sons or another close family member! Had we gone into the market and purchased a live goat, chicken or duck and taken that onto the bus, no problem. Life isn't fair.

It proved to us that you don't have to spend a fortune to have a good day's fishing but at the same time, we knew that the bamboo rods were only going to work when fishing close in. Our Diawa rods and reels would still have their use and one place we knew they would work was the Sembawang fishing ponds. This was the first time we had ever fished at this type of venue and there were strict rules on the baits, hook sizes, return policy, etc. Both Ray and I and our younger brother Graeme managed to catch fish here and it was worth the visit. The one single thing that stands out for me was watching the Chinese boy who was fishing next to me. Time and again I would be getting great bites only to see him landing big fish with what appeared to be little effort on his part. He appeared to be casting out and winding in without delay and I slowly became frustrated with his success and my dwindling catch rate. I got to the point where I convinced myself that it was either his better tackle set-up or choice of bait that was paying dividends. As any fisherman will tell you, under these circumstances, it calls for a spying mission. I went to have a chat with him just as he was winding in another of 'my fish'. In absolute amazement, I saw that it was nothing to do with the bait he was using, there wasn't any! Apart from the weight on his line, all that was present was a string of treble-hooks. He was foul hooking fish that were going for my bait! I couldn't believe it. Our day's fishing at Sembawang was soon to be over.

**Kevin Daley remembers:**
**Sembawang fishing ponds. Ray & Kev's trophies.**
**What is it with older brothers? He fishes with a shorter rod and still catches a bigger fish than mine!**

My brother loved fishing too when we lived in Malaya. Most of his catches also came from along by the Skudai. I can't remember that we ever ate any of them, they were probably snapped up by a local cat!

More Tiger Beer! Here's a photo of the Paradise Bar and restaurant. Ron Spurrier is on the right.

Ron Spurrier on the left. Is that another glass of Tiger Beer?

The Nelson Bar, Sembawang 1970.

Inside the Nelson Bar,Sembawang,1970.

Harbour Telok Ayer Basin.
Now called Telok Ayer Wharves. During the 1960s, it was quite a busy harbour. It now forms part of an upmarket development known as Marina Bay. This includes the nearby Marina Mall and has its own MRT station.

Harbour Telok Ayer Basin.
The area was built on reclaimed land. Originally, the Thian Hock Keng Temple was by the waterside but after reclamation, it found itself five blocks away from the river.

Fishing under a parasol 1970.
I'm sure everyone recalls the smell of these Wanchai Burberrys, the name for the paper and bamboo parasols, especially once they were wet.

Fishing hut 1970.

Lion dance costume.

Lion dances were popular in Singapore and mainly took part in Chinese populated parts of the city. The dance dates back 1,500 years and is meant to bring wealth and good fortune. They can sometime be seen during the opening of new buildings and shops but more often at Chinese New Year.

**Clive Baker remembers:**
**I can't find any photos of Sembawang, which was my personal favourite local run-ashore but these photos of Nee Soon Village somehow survived the test of time. The Pongos (Army) inhabited Nee Soon Garrison so it was generally thought impolite by Jack to invade their territory, steal their women and drink them under the table. However the dhobi wallas in Nee Soon laundry really cleaned up in Terror (no pun intended).**

# Six
# The People

It was interesting to see all the different people that inhabited Singapore. These included Chinese, Indians and Malays. Until we arrived in Singapore, I had never seen anyone wearing a turban and as a kid, I was fascinated by them.

People that stand out in my mind are the ice cream seller who drove his motor scooter van type contraption to our house every day, the snake charmers and magicians in the heart of Singapore, our lovely amah, our landlord, Swan Singh, who wore a turban and had curled shoes, the street sellers, the Satay man and the grass cutters who used huge scythes that they swung over their heads.

The Gully Gully man.

The Gully Gully man was a sort of street magician who used snakes and baby chickens in his act. The snakes were meant to have the poison taken out of them before they were brought into contact with members of the public but there were still some, like me, that were reluctant to go anywhere near them! The Gully Gully man would also perform tricks with hankies, rubber balls and metal rings. A baby chick would be placed under three metal cups, moved around and you had to guess which one it was under. Of course, it never was in the one you thought it was going to be!

The Gully Gully man with a snake, 1964.

Snakes around shoulders, 1964. I had this done to me but I wasn't so calm as these kids! I was mesmerised by the Gully Gully men who use to perform their magic on the streets of Singapore particularly near to the Raffles Hotel and also by Tiger Balm Gardens.

A man taking part in a Thaipusam festival. The festival was celebrated by Hindus, mostly in the Tamil community, on the full moon in the Tamil month of Thai. They were pretty shocking to see and I think it was one festival that we avoided. Being small at the time, I think it would have given me nightmares. My brother may have gone though.

# Seven

# Tiger Balm Gardens

Tiger Balm Gardens was located on Pasir Panjang Road. I would always look forward to visiting. I loved all the statues especially the ones of animals and even more so, the ones you could climb on! The statues were huge to me then, especially the huge gorillas and the laughing Buddha. The ornamental gateway will stick in many people's memories as will the two fighting Sumo wrestlers and the statue of the Chinese dancing lady. There must be hundreds of photos around similar to ours, all featuring these well remembered exhibits.

In 1985, Tiger Balm Gardens was converted into an amusement park and many of the old statues, that we knew and loved, disappeared and were replaced with funfair type rides. This would explain why, when I went back in 1990, that the giant gorilla which was so popular with many kids in the 1960s had disappeared. A charge was also introduced to get in. However, after its conversion, the park lost money drastically. To try and regain its once popularity, the park owners have now replaced many of the original statues and removed the funfair rides and it's now open free to the public.

**Clive Baker remembers:**
**Tiger Balm Gardens was a delight, full of grotesque alabaster statues in all stages of contortion and depicting the most horrific physical mayhem that the locals must have indulged in in some period of their history. There is another Tiger Balm Gardens in Hong Kong which also has happy memories for me but I won't get into that! Somewhere I have loads of colour photos of the exhibits adorned by drunken sailors in various states of undress. I wonder where they all are now?**

The lower entrance to Tiger Balm Gardens before you reached the Tiger Pagoda. In the 1960s, the roads leading up to the gardens were lined with snake charmers playing flutes to enchant cobras from cane baskets. There were also acrobats performing amazing feats and public plays were put on to promote Chinese Culture.

Alan, mum and me at Tiger Balm Gardens. Below were all the animals that we loved playing on. On the left are a couple of strange wombat like creatures and also a turtle.

My brother Alan and my mum in a corner of the gardens.

Two photos near the centre of the gardens with three statues of old wise
Chinese men. A pagoda stands in the background.

John Harper and his brothers. The gorilla features in many of our photos
and was a popular attraction.

The laughing Buddha.
It was meant to bring you luck if you rubbed his belly.

The pagoda leading up into the gardens. Tiger Balm Gardens also included the Ten Courts of Hell which featured gruesome statues depicting hideous punishments for things as simple as lying or gambling. The punishments featured were pretty severe too. If you were caught swearing or cheating, your body would be sawn in half and thrown onto a bed of knives! It's always been a popular exhibit at the gardens but I gave it a miss when I was a kid so that I could sleep at night!

A statue of a Chinese samurai complete with sword.

This statue of Confucius was brightly coloured and his cloak was painted blue. The statues have now been repainted and appear even more brightly painted than they were originally.

My brother and me trying to escape from the gardens on a hippopotamus!
These animals were in the fenced off area.

Another smaller smiling Buddha statue.

The Sumo Wrestlers at the beginning of the park.

A close up photo of one of the Sumo wrestlers.

The large pagoda in the middle of the gardens, 1963.

A statue of a wise old Chinese man points the way.

The many statues that were in the part of the park you were meant to keep out of. In the foreground is a giant lobster and in the background, a turtle and two walruses. I remember playing on them all and there's a photo of me and my brother sat on the turtle in my previous book.

# Eight

# The Botanic Gardens

All kids loved going to the Singapore Botanic Gardens just to see the monkeys. They seemed to be everywhere and everyone would always stock up on bananas before they went in. The gardens had several entrances; Tanglin Gate, Burkill Gate, Nassim Gate and Cluny Park Gate, and there was also entry through the Bukit Timah entrance.

Sir Stamford Raffles, a keen naturalist, established the first Botanical Garden at Government Hill in 1822 but it was closed in 1829, after Raffles death, due to lack of funding. The present gardens were founded in 1859 by an agri-horticultural society and were planned as a leisure and ornamental garden.

Famous at one time for the monkeys, they've all now, unfortunately, been removed. I remember them well as does Kevin Daley with the next few pictures.

A mother and her baby at the Botanic Gardens.

**Kevin Daley remembers:**
**From an early age, babies are taught to steal nuts, wrist watches and jewellery.**

**Kevin Daley remembers:**
**It was shortly after this photo was taken that one of the monkeys**
**tried to remove the wrist watch!**

**Kevin Daley remembers:**
**The paper cone of nuts looks safe behind Graeme's back but not for**
**long!**

**Kevin Daley remembers:**
**From here, we could see an enormous fish hiding under the lily**
**pads.**

Two local girls in front of a working floral clock within the Botanic Gardens.
The floral clock is still there and is located in the Sundial Gardens.

Taking it easy 1970.

Children in the Botanic Gardens, 1970.

# Nine
# Amahs and
# Amah's Markets

Most servicemen's families employed an amah. She would help out with
the cooking, cleaning and would also look after the children
All the kids loved their Amah and many saw her as a second mother.

Alan Cottrell's family's amah, Ah Yong, taken in 1965.

**Vivien Webster remembers:**
**I remember someone very special to me, our amah, Wong Thye**
**Heng.**
**When Thye Heng first came to work for us, she told us her name was**
**Esther. She couldn't pronounce this 'Christian' name very well and**
**one wonders who gave her that name originally and why. So we**
**used her Chinese name. Some time later, we discovered she didn't**
**like her Chinese name much either as, apparently, it is a male name -**
**wishful thinking on her father's behalf perhaps.**
**She looked all of 17, but was in fact in her late twenties. Thye Heng**
**has the misfortune to be born 6th or 7th daughter in a large family.**
**When she was 4 or 5, she was sold by her father to two Chinese**
**women. These women trained her to be a domestic and then sent her**
**out to work and collected her wages. She never attended school and**
**did not know how to read or write. This was the 'home' she**

returned to at weekends. She had trouble with my name too (Vivien), as the V sound is not used in Chinese languages, and so I was 'Missy'. I understand this was common practice amongst amahs. My mother taught Thye Heng how to play cards, which she loved, and how to read the ingredients in a recipe. She always had the radio on in the kitchen and I remember her practising her Mandarin. She spoke English, Malay and her own Chinese dialect but it was at this time that Lee Kuan Yew introduced the Speak Mandarin Campaign. When we were due to return to Oz, she gave my mother a quilt that she worked on at night during her time with us. That quilt has become something of an heirloom in our family.

After we left Singapore, Thye Heng stopped working at the base and worked for a Canadian diplomat. We did keep in touch with her for quite a few years, although knowing she had to pay a letter-writer to read our letters to her, and to write hers, made us feel a little uncomfortable.

During our time in Singapore, Thye Heng became very much a part of our family and something of a big sister to me. Although 'uneducated', she was very wise in the ways of the world. There are times when I think of her and remember her sayings and part of Thye Heng will always remain with me.

Gem traders at an Amah's market, 1970.

David Robbins remembers:
The market street was called the 'Amah's Market'. Amah is the Malay name for a domestic maid. Traditionally, the amahs would go shopping at one of these after work looking for cheaper goods than

they would find in the stores. There seemed to be everything on earth for sale on the lamp lit tables. Watches, shoes, clothes, vegetables and fruit that we had never seen before, jewellery and even live chickens.

'Look at the people, where did they all come from?' asked my mum. We looked around and the long line of stalls were fast becoming crowded. It seemed that as soon as the sun went down, waiting throngs of shoppers appeared out of nowhere and headed straight for the street looking for bargains. I was enthralled with the different languages spoken by customers at the stalls. Some were high pitched and sounded excited, others were deep and growling.

'Look at all the insects!' I said.

Clouds of flying creatures, some a few inches long, buzzed and flitted around the lamps hanging in front of the stalls. John and I walked as close to one of the swarms as we thought wise. Huge winged ants, green looking beetles, tiny insects and long ones, surrounded the bright lights from the lanterns.

Shirt traders 1970.

**Brian Mitchell remembers:**

The very first record I ever bought, a 45rpm single, was Paul Anka's hit song, 'Diana'. I bought it soon after I arrived in Singapore at a night-time market which must have been on or near the Orchard Estate where I lived for a short while. I recall the busy market stalls lit by gas or kerosene lamps and it was one of my first experiences of buying at a market. I probably had to haggle over the price which I always hated doing! Shopping in Singapore for us Brits was always an adventure, in the UK you hardly ever got the chance to haggle over price.

130

A gem trader, 1970.

A Chinese lady selling her wares, 1970.

# Ten

# The Woodlands Naval Base and HMS Terror

Many of our dads worked at the Naval Base in Sembawang. My dad worked there as a Chief Petty Officer at KD Malaya. We spent quite a lot of time at the Naval Base as there was always something going on there for Naval families. I remember the great firework displays to celebrate Chinese New Year, the outdoor movie shows and all the events that seemed to be laid on for the kids. Christmas was another great time and we all loved waiting for the Naval Base Santa Claus to get our Christmas presents.

Canberra Gate was one of the main gates into the Naval Base at Sembawang. Other entrances included Rotheram Gate and the Sembawang Main Gate.

Clive Baker remembers:
There were several, I can't remember how many, of these imposing accommodation blocks in Terror. Of course, in those days, there was no air conditioning to speak of, apart from windows and doors flung wide open and the occasional overhead fan which kept you awake all night, unless you had had a skin full of Tiger beer that is!
These blocks, or messes, were where Jack, sometimes, slept when his ship was in the Dockyard for a refit, or waiting for 'Jenny's side party' to finish painting the ships side.
In those days, ships used to be away from home for up to two years and quite often at sea for 3 months at a stretch, so it was considered a holiday to be based here for a while. However, payday could never come soon enough as the local temptations were awesome, money lenders thrived and many a poor matelot didn't pay off his debts for months after a brief sojourn here.
As a member of Terror Ship's Company, I had to regulate my spending if I was to survive for a year or two, so I found a lucrative way of earning more cash by taking photos at all the ship's major functions so that Jack could send them home to mum. As an extension of this moonlight activity, I formed the Royal Navy Photographic Club (Singapore) with the aid of a generous donation from the Captain's Welfare Fund! It helped to pass those long hot days, I guess.

**Clive Baker remembers:**
The main entrance to HMS Terror, with it's original muzzle loaders
which would have been a chief GI's dream, was situated nearly at the
end of the main road from Singapore City. This road ran from the
Johore Causeway right into Singapore, passing many villages and
plantations on the way. It was a tortuous drive in one of the many
Mercedes taxis that plied their trade between Bugis Street and the
Naval Base just down the road. Mind you, I can't remember many
drives back to base, they usually ended up in Sembawang village,
from where we staggered back to Terror, mostly on our knees!

Clive Baker remembers:
The Regulating Office. This is the building that you tried to avoid. A Naval Police Station, this is where you went if you had too many Tiger Beers the night before and ended up staying overnight in the infamous Bugis Street (now sadly reformed I am told) and arriving back on board half an hour adrift.

Kevin Daley remembers:
I had one meeting with a monitor that got the heart racing. My father was a submariner and whenever HMS Rorqual was at home we often went to HMS Terror. On one visit my dad took delivery of a hand built 2-man canoe and he and my older brother set off from the pier next to HMS Forth, the submarine depot ship. I was left waiting for my turn on the pier, holding the spare paddle. They paddled off and were some way away from me when I started to hear a strange hissing noise coming from below the pier structure. There on the rocks, heading towards me was a very large monitor lizard, its tail swaying from side to side. It was big and mean and constantly flicking its tongue.
'Dad!'
*DDAADD!*
DDDDDAAAAADDDDD!!
I didn't get to paddle that day, it seemed like a bad idea.

**Clive Baker remembers:**
**A féte in Terror was a periodical thing that the ship's purser laid on to mainly placate the local dignitaries. We didn't mind the poncing about so much because the beer and scran were free!**

My parents, on the right, with Les and Bette Sharp at a party at
KD Malaya.

Ron Spurrier on the balcony of one of the accommodation blocks at HMS
Terror in 1963. The swimming pool is in the background.

The Naval Base Brownies.
Deanna Morton, Gill Wrenn, Margaret Mee ( I think her Mum was the
Brown Owl) Julie Crapnell, and possibly Jennifer Murdoch and Marion
Randall. Jennifer Boyce is in the front row, first on the left.
Christabelle Alvis was the Guide Commissioner and the photo was taken
outside St. Peter's Church, probably around 1960.

**Dee Hinton remembers:**
**I remember the teenage gatherings at the swimming pool on the top
lawn by the changing rooms. It was always our domain. Listening to
the Rolling Stones singing, 'Under the Boardwalk' as we sat around
in the sun eating chips and tomato sauce and drinking coke with a
slice of lemon and lots of ice.**
**I recall Mrs Morse, the fearsome swimming teacher, whose speedy
remedy for non swimmers was to throw you in and see what
happened! To be fair, I don't think she was that bad but it is how I
remember her as a child and she certainly took that approach with at
least one child. She may well have had other reasons. I learnt to do
swallow dives into the waiting arms of Lt Cdr Meredith RN, the Head
at the Naval Base Junior School ( I have the picture to prove it). Poor
man would probably be arrested for such in this day and age. He
also believed in the boys fighting with gloves on in a ring watched
by the rest of us if they were caught fighting in the playground. I
remember Mr Nutter and Mr Bird who also taught us there.**

Naval Base teenagers in the Teenage Room at The Dockyard Club.
November 1966.

**Dee Hinton remembers:**
**I recall the dances at the Dockyard Club with MJB and The Talismen**
**and the Teenage Room underneath the Club where we had hours of**
**fun and where the boys formed a band, 'The Shapes'. I still see two**
**of them at the twice yearly reunions in London. I also remember**
**banyans, St Andrew's Youth Club (still in touch with Bill Inglis who**
**was the young Naval Officer who used to run it for a while. Many**
**remember his little MG).**
**Also, I remember a totally mad charity football match which the**
**teenagers organised on the sports ground behind the swimming**
**club. Think I may have the newspaper clipping somewhere with Sue**
**Le Maux (still around and contactable) running with the ball. It turned**
**out to be a cross between rugby and football!**

A shot of the HMS Terror Block.

**Ellen Tait remembers:**
**Once through the Naval Gate, we came to Sembawang with its small interesting shops. They would make a dress the same day for $2.50, about 6 shillings in English money. They would also make the kids' sandals for school. It was also the cheapest place to have suits made. In the evenings, the outside would change and eating stalls would be set up, Nasi Goren was our favourite !**

Armada Club Naafi 1970.

Two shots of the Minerva Gala 1970.

HMS Minerva Gala 1970.

Senior rates pool, 1970

HMS Terror at night time.

# Eleven

# RAF Tengah

RAF Tengah was the Air Force station situated at Choa Chu Kang Road
on the North West of the island. The base was commissioned in 1939.
When Singapore gained its independence, it became the Republic of
Singapore Air Force and is known now as Tengah Airbase.

81 Squadron Buildings 1960

**Vivien Webster remembers:**
**We lived in Sycamore Crescent at Tengah from early 1977 to late
1979, from the time I was 14 until I was 16. Some of my memories
are, again, our wonderful amah, Thye Heng, who we loved and didn't
want to leave behind, her saying 'different people, different ways' will
never leave me.**
**I remember the 'Youth Group' (disco) on Friday nights at Tengah
School, the walk to the swimming pool where you had to go across
the end of the runway and felt like ducking when the fighters were
taking off, not being able to hear a thing when they warmed the
engines at night, the Indian movies on Singapore TV (hilarious!),
madly filling up the bath when we got the call that the water pipes
had broken further up the line, the time when an American plane, I
think a C141 Starlifter, had to land at Tengah. It was gigantic and**

everyone came out to have a look, although the SAF were running around telling us that we couldn't see anything – a bit like when they transported their missiles on a truck under a huge tarp and you weren't supposed to know what it was! I also recall going for rides with my dad on a motorbike amongst the kampongs, Xmas concerts and the melodrama (boo, hiss), the 'cooee' competition on Australia Day, the ANZAC dawn service at Kranji, so poignant, and then drinking a glass of rum with some Australian Navy guys, the suicide rate when they started shifting villagers from kampongs into the high rise buildings – if they took their shoes off, then they had jumped and weren't pushed, playing golf in the dark on New Year's Eve, being terrified of walking anywhere barefoot in case you got hookworm, playing lots of tennis and then the huge Coke that Sunny would serve up to us at the Golf Club afterwards, Dad throwing things at the geckos (chit chats) on the ceiling if they started mating! Hello to the Mortimers (we went on holiday to Tioman Island with you guys) and also the Aldersons who lived down the street from us. I played tennis with a girl called Glenda who went to school in NZ but came to Singapore during the holidays, her sister Joanne and I think her brother lived close to us. If anyone remembers the Kneebones, I would love to catch up with Steven, Anthony or Teresa. Babysat a lot of kids at Tengah, especially remember David Kennett, such a great kid!

The pool viewed from Ward Block. Two people are tending the grass.

Tony Arrowsmith (in uniform) outside Ward Block in 1960

View of RAF Tengah from billet 1960.

The front entrance, complete with improvised oil drums marked 'Keep Left!', 1963.

Tengah Mess.

The pool, 1963.

The McGregor Club, 1963.

# Twelve

# Banyans

Everyone loved going on banyans. It was great getting on a hired boat and going off to an island or deserted beach somewhere. There was always one or more barbeques on the go. My dad's use to weigh a ton but he still took it. Sometimes, he'd just make one out of some old bricks and cook on there. Everyone was involved and would have a great time. Often, a huge parachute would be spread out between cars and people would shelter beneath it to keep out of the sun.

Me on a boat heading for a banyan. I probably don't look too happy because I had just lost my fishing line over the side! I never did catch anything anyway!
I remember one banyan where we arrived at what appeared to be a deserted island. The tide had recently gone out and there were starfish all over the sand.

**Ellen Tait remembers:**
**One of our favourite trips out was at the weekends. Les Sharp, who was a diver, had the use of a boat and a crowd of us would go on a banyan to a deserted beach, taking barbeque stuff with us. We had an old parachute that we managed to drape around for shade. We had a go at water skiing which was great until you had to let go then you thought of all the 'nasties' lurking beneath and wished the boat would hurry back!**

**Kevin Daley remembers: A banyan with HMS Rorqual on 24th Sept 1967. We always looked forward to the banyans. Paula Ubin Island seemed to be the favourite place to go.**

That red bucket looks familiar. Could it be one of those that you always got free with the washing powder? We always took ours to the beach too!

Ron Spurrier on a beach near Singapore with a home made barbeque.
The fire is made out of a few coconut husks and palm tree leaves while a
kettle is put on to boil. Ron is lighting a cigarette using a cooking utensil.

There was always lots to do for kids at a banyan. We'd go swimming, play
football or just explore. Someone always had a lilo and there were plenty
of snorkels and masks for seeing the fish underwater. There was always a
barbeque going so there was always plenty to eat.

Ron Spurrier, in hat, taking part in the tug of war, 1963. There were lots of beach activities during the banyans. Adults would play cricket, football, badminton and even go water skiing. There was also plenty of Tiger Beer on hand for all the men.

Ron Spurrier in the middle with his hat on, 1963.

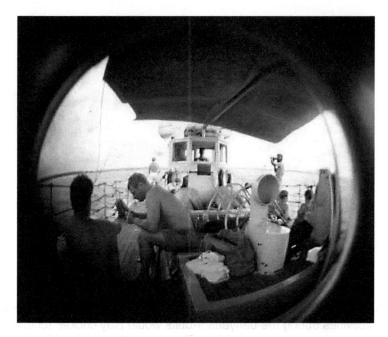

On the way to a banyan on the HMS Minerva, 1970.

Above, some of the crew of the HMS Minerva enjoying a banyan in
August 1970.

Above and below, some of the HMS Minerva crew 1970.
Below, cooling off in the sea with a few cans of Tiger Beer.

# Thirteen

# School

School days in Singapore and Malaya will always be remembered by all of us probably because we only had to go until 1pm and also because of the hot, tropical weather and the time spent outdoors. Oh, and also because of the strawberry and chocolate flavoured milk!
There were several now famous people at various schools in Singapore and Malaya at the time and perhaps you remember some of them? These included Jenny Agutter, Joanna Lumley, Anne Widdecombe, Pam Ayres, Paul Greenwood (who played the policeman, Rosie), John Inverdale, a page 3 girl called Stephanie Jenkins, Eve Stratford, a Bunny girl (who was unfortunately murdered) and even martial arts expert, Steven Segal. I wonder if he got all his ideas from watching episodes of Samurai?

The School Bus, 1958.

**Colin McCormac remembers:**
**1958 was just after Merdeka (Freedom from Britain) and there was still a worry about a backlash and terrorism, so we had our wired in truck with an armed Ghurka at the door to protect us. As an 11 year old I didn't see anything strange about that at all!**

Peter Banks receiving an end of year class prize from Mr Harry Fulthorpe (Dockyard Chief Constructor) at the 'Japanese' Theatre in the Base.

**Kevin Daley remembers:**
**Once I had left the Junior school, I was enrolled at Bourne school in Singapore. I assume that as the population of military families grew, it proved a challenge to the education authority. As a result, Bourne school was split into two sections, quite a distance apart. I remember that most of our lessons were 'doubles' and some took place in Alexandra and others in Gillman. This resulted in us having to take buses between schools. A unique experience for most school children, I guess. Another unique feature was that from time to time, we would see the odd snake going over the pathways that linked the school buildings.**

**Gill Pennock remembers: I loved the New Zealand milk we got at morning recess at primary school in Singapore. For whatever reason, we didn't seem to be able to get Australian dairy items very often and always had NZ dairy - fernleaf butter, fresh or flavoured milk, cheese, yummo!**
**I remember frozen cordial in flasks with hand towels wrapped around them, that dates back to the RN school days (pre-Woodlands). How many flasks did we break each week?**

155

On the Naval School playing field. Malcolm Banks is sitting nearest to the camera, taken in July 1959.

This photo was taken on the HMS Terror sports ground. Peter Banks is in the sack furthest from the camera.

John Harper remembers:

Forces' schools in Singapore were modelled on the education system in the UK with Primary schools from age 5 to age 11 and Secondary schools from age 11 to age 15, 16 or 18 depending on the level of dedication and attainment. The Secondary system was split into two, the more academic would go to the 'Grammar' school whilst the less academic would be given an education that was focused more towards practical skills but with a degree of academic requirement as well. These were known as the 'Modern' schools. Which type of school you attended was determined at the age of 11 by the 11 plus examination. This included tests on mathematical ability, comprehension and IQ testing of the type where you had to identify the next number in various sequences, sometimes arithmetic, sometimes geometric in progression. Reasoning tests were also there with strange items to solve like the odd one out in a series of pictures say like a square, a rectangle, a triangle and a circle, with the circle being the odd one out because it is not made up of straight lines. There were also reasoning tests like 'man is to hat as dustbin is to...' a whole list of things that included 'lid'. You were meant to choose lid because it goes on top like a hat goes on top of a man.

Arriving in Singapore just after my tenth birthday meant that the 11 plus was the very next thing for me to face when I went up to the final year of primary school. My mother had worried about my school abilities whilst we had lived in Cleveleys and had even gone to ask my form teacher about extra tuition and coaching so that I would be able to pass the eleven plus. She was told in no uncertain terms that that would never happen, as service families are just not worth bothering with as they are always moving on. So, it came as a welcome surprise to my mother that a lot of effort was put in by service schools to get pupils up to speed and practised for the eleven plus. The pace was quite pushed and we were set exercises to be done under timed conditions. I can remember we would no sooner have finished a set of arithmetic questions than we would be going on to some of the IQ questions. It was really a hothouse environment for coaching scholars to be able to pass the eleven plus.

Being a part of the post war baby boom or 'part of a statistical bulge', there had always been accommodation problems for every class I had been in with either extra desks needed or an extra classroom having to be conjured up from somewhere. Changi was no exception and when I arrived my class was over in the three-story block across the playground in the Secondary school.

For the final year at Primary school a new block was built for us just round the corner from the Anglican Church. Because it was intended to be only temporary, it was built of wood and thatched in attap palm leaves. There was a bit of indignation at this but this soon simmered down once we got into the buildings as we found that they were a lot cooler than the brick built buildings of the main part of the school. They also had a spacious and airy feel about them. They also seemed to be a lot quieter and I am sure that this helped to contribute to the air of industry in that final year as we prepared to take the dreaded eleven plus. School was six mornings a week and it was compulsory to attend at least two afternoon activities per week. I looked through the list of options and decided that swimming was a must, as I wanted to improve on my basic achievement of learning to swim in the first two weeks of arriving in Singapore. The second activity I chose was called the 'Malaya Club'. Here we learnt about the Federation of Malay states and about some of the trees and plant life. It was during these lessons that I was first introduced to 'pitcher' plants in the form of the Raffles Pitcher Plant which, I understand, if you find any in Singapore now you are not allowed to pick them. Even today, I think that they are fascinating plants. During these lessons we were also introduced to the Hibiscus and some of it's herbal properties. We often used them to make hot poultices, I once had a septic spot on the palm of my hand where I had fallen onto some mimosa and got a thorn stuck. When it turned septic, it was straight out and gather up some hibiscus flowers, pour on boiling water then slap the poultice onto the infection to draw it out. It very quickly cleared up with this treatment. I had suggested this treatment to my mother after hearing about it in the 'Malaya Club'. We were also introduced to number of other trees including the fragrant 'Frangipani'. Frangipani are amongst my favourite trees, maybe because I can recognise them easily, but also because of the fragrance which is sweet and heady.
My swimming progressed well and I soon reached the stage of taking the beginner's certificate which entailed swimming a length of the pool (33 yards) breaststroke and crawl. Then I worked up to the advanced which included 3 lengths of breaststroke, 3 lengths of crawl, a length of backstroke and a dive from the side of the pool followed by a dive from the 10-ft high board (about 3 metres for you metric youngsters).
The eleven plus exam was looming, we had moved house by this time, from Lloyd Leas to Wittering Road on the main part of the camp near to Changi Village. I was promised that if I passed the exam, I would get a bicycle as a reward!

158

The Royal Naval School bus

It was then that we found out that as well as the eleven plus examination, we would also be sitting the Scottish equivalent called the Moray House exam. This was in case any of our parents were posted to Scotland on their return to the UK. The exam days came and went and didn't seem all that stressful. It was my first experience of being herded into a large hall full of desks with very stern and official looking invigilators, a large clock on the wall to show how much time you had used. Some found it intimidating but we had been coached so well most of our class just sat down and worked through the papers like it was a normal classroom exercise. Once the exam was over, I then began to worry as to what would happen if I passed one exam and not the other. Would I still get that bike? I so desperately wanted that bike. It turned out that I need not have worried as I had passed both exams. So, I got my first bike. I went down to Changi Village with my dad and we had a look at what was on offer and found one to fit me. It was a German cycle called Heiko. It was of the 'sit up and beg' variety as most bikes were in those days with pull up brakes. Learning to ride it was, of course, another story.
At this point I should have been moving on to Changi Grammar but

The Royal Naval School infants, 1963

my father was posted to RAF Tengah on the other side of the island. There was only a primary school at Tengah and so we were taken by bus to Alexandra Grammar School at Gillman Barracks close to the city. Each day became a well practised routine, my mother would wake me at about 6 am each morning and I would get up, wash and dress, make up some milk for my breakfast and for my younger brothers who were still asleep. Then breakfast would be a couple of Weet Bix biscuits with milk and some coffee made with Carnation evaporated milk. I can't stand the taste of it nowadays but when it was all you get, you had to get used to it. I would put Radio Malaya on to listen to the start of the day's programmes which always started with 'oh what a beautiful morning, oh what a beautiful day'. At the point where he sings about elephants eyes, the bus would be passing our house up to the top of Meteor Road. At the top, the bus would turn round and start picking up. From Meteor Road we would head across the light controlled runway sometimes having to stop for Canberras and Venoms taking off laden with armaments. This was during the time of the 'Malayan Emergency' when the communist insurgents were being dealt with. The UK government didn't want to call it war after having spent so long at war, hence the term 'Emergency'. From there, we proceeded along what is now the Choa Chu Kang Road towards Bukit Panjang and then turned right towards Bukit Timah. Along the way, we would pass the 'Metal Box' and 'Ford' factories picking up some more passengers at Foo Yong estate just before we got to Bukit Timah. From there, we would make a small detour off Bukit Timah Road to pick up an officer's daughter and then proceed back onto Bukit Timah Road down to Newton Circus and exit onto Scotts Road until we reached Orchard Road. On the corner of Orchard Road, there were always magnificent posters for films at the Shaw Brothers Cinema. The most remarkable was the poster for 'The Vikings'. I didn't get to see this film until some years later when we returned to the UK. From Orchard Road, the bus would take us along Tanglin Road and then turn on to Alexandra Road driving past the Archipelago Brewery. Once we had passed the British Military Hospital (BMH), with its distinctive cross of St George painted on the roof, we knew we were almost there. I think the hospital is now known as Alexandra Hospital. Just after the hospital was a bend and then a left turn into Depot Road where we would be dropped off to walk up the hill to Alexandra Grammar School whilst the bus carried on to the Alexandra Modern School.

Most days the journey would be uneventful, there was a sing song along the way with all the Scout favourites like 'You'll never go to heaven' (on an RAF bus, cos an RAF bus, wont take all of us.). Popular songs of the day like The Everly Brothers', 'Wake Up Little Suzie', and Elvis Presley's, 'Teddy Bear' and 'Wont You Wear My Ring Around Your Neck' were also firm favourites. In 1959, there had been a long period without rain and one day the Prime Minister, Lee Kuan Yew, announced that if it didn't rain soon, drought measures would have to be put in place. Well, of course it started to rain early that morning and it just kept on raining heavily. On the way back home, the bus was brought to a standstill by the floodwaters near the biscuit factory. We were stuck there for a long time. Eventually the waters subsided enough for the bus to get through. When we got to Bukit Timah Road, the canal that runs between Bukit Timah Road and Dunearn had overflowed its banks and the people that lived in tents alongside the banks were trying to dry out their few meagre belongings.

At AGS, I was introduced to science. As well as the General Science lessons, we also had some lessons called Applied Science. I find it hard to put into words the thrill I found in science. The general science looked at some chemical reactions and the differences between mixtures and compounds. There was also some physics in there, looking at the expansion of metals when heated. The applied science covered topics like electromagnetism and how bells and solenoids worked, transformers, microphones and telephones and how batteries worked. There was even a visit to the telephone exchange where we could see all these applications at work. This was a subject that I could get wrapped up in and at the Christmas exam time I managed a score of 98%. This was indeed the start of a passionate and lifelong interest in science and the application of science.

At the start of the autumn term, we were more or less assigned to forms in date order of our applications. Because of the move from Changi to Tengah I was down at the bottom of the list and ended up in form 1F. The Christmas exams were used to grade us and I moved up to class 1B. Despite having a wonderful memory for all sorts of things, I cannot recall the names of any of the people in form 1B. However, from form 1F, I do remember a Graham Miller but that is probably because I met him a few years later in the UK on a canoeing course.

Sport was never my forte. I hated gymnastics and even smacked my head trying to do a handspring. I guess I was just basically clumsy. I also hated running, though the cross country runs we used to do took us on a route out the back of the school and onto the hilltop and around a small Kampong before heading back to school. The runs were only short as we didn't have much time and the heat made it hard work. Swimming was a completely different matter and we always had a least one lesson a week at the swimming pool. In water, I guess I was like the ugly duckling transformed into a swan. I was very fast at breast stroke and was picked to train for the school team. I attended the first week's training but there was no RAF transport back to Tengah. There were three of us from Tengah and we managed to persuade the bus from the Naval Base to take us and drop us off in Bukit Panjang. From there, we walked a little way over the level crossing and maybe walked for about fifteen minutes before somebody stopped and gave us a lift. When I got home my mother hit the roof and put her foot down saying that if there was no transport back to Tengah then I was not going to be attending the training sessions. So, that finished my promising start as a competitive swimmer. Well, that meant I could enjoy swimming without having to put in all that rigorous training.

AGS was where I first experienced learning a foreign language formally for the first time. In the first year, we were introduced to French. I found it fascinating though I was never good at French, I was probably in that band of scholars that hovers around the middle, neither doing well but not doing badly. One of the French teachers was a Madame Hook and I am sure that she used to wear a cape to school and seemed a very strange woman. Maybe I dreamed up that bit about the cape, I'll have to check with my friend Raymond Clayton to confirm that.

**Form 1B had the disadvantage of having a distracting view out to the approaches to the harbour. I do remember being distracted sometimes by the large ships passing by particularly if the lessons were getting a bit heavy.**

Teachers at the Kebunteh Naval School in Malaya, 1960s. I was there at the same time but can't remember any of them! The classrooms were around the sides and the entrance to the school was behind where the teachers are. I remember catching the bus home from there, at the end of the lessons, especially the trip where the driver got lost and we all ended up in the wrong place!

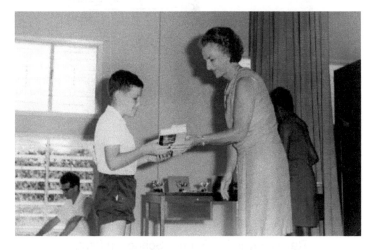

Alan Tait receiving 'Stirring Stories for Boys' at the Royal Naval School at Kebunteh in Malaya.

**Steve Burnett remembers:**
I remember going to school in Raeburn Park in Singapore centre more or less , a primary school I went to after the forces left RAF Changi. We used to get picked up by one of the brown and yellow taxis and driven all the way. Some days, my dads chauffeur would pick us up! It seemed totally normal but reflecting it sounds privileged , even though all ex pats had gardeners, amahs, and drivers. One day, I came home from school and my mother told me she found a lump in my bed. She peeked under the bedspread and saw a snake coiled up at the foot of it. It turned out it was a python looking for somewhere warm to sleep. My mum was always freaked out by the bugs and beasties in Singapore. Anyway, she got the gardener to come in and get it , he managed to pick it up with the end of a boom and he released it into the jungle area at the back of our house.

**Dee Hinton remembers:**
I remember my white starched pique uniform when I was at the Naval Base School and my short green skirts when at St John's. I also recall the church parade with the Brownies and Guides and carrying the colours. I remember learning how to fold a flag correctly so that it would unfurl when we hoisted it and the singing of songs on the RN buses at the end of term and the rolls of toilet paper that used to be hung out of the window to see how long a piece one could fly!

Ray Daley in his Bourne School uniform.

Graeme Daley's class at Kebunteh Junior School.

Sports Day at Kebunteh Royal Naval Junior School on 19th July 1967. Robert Bagwell is at the front in a black t shirt and Kevin Daley is 3rd in the line.

# Fourteen
# Malaya
## Johore Bahru

We loved living at Jalan Wijaya in Johore Bahru. All the service people
just knew it as 'JB'. It was close enough to Singapore to travel in by car or
on the bus across the causeway. It was a bit quieter than the main city.

**Ellen Tait remembers:**
**I still remember the awful smell of the Durian fruit, it was supposed
to taste great but the smell put us off! All of Jalan Ahfook didn't
smell very  sweet. I think it was partly to do with the market there
and the heat. We named it 'Sweet Water Canal'! At night, outside the
market and all the way along Jalan Ahfook, the shopkeepers just
opened up their canvas beds and slept outside their shops. They
didn't seem to suffer from insect bites like the rest of us. I think they
had them trained to just bite the foreigners!**
**The first week out there, I had Alan and Derek with me and we saw
what looked like a float for a carnival. It was very  colourful, covered
in flowers and pictures with lots of singing and chanting and
dancing around. I picked Derek up to see it  and took Alan's hand,
and said, 'Lets watch the parade!'.**
**We were enjoying it until someone said, 'You're not watching a
parade - it's a funeral!'.**

Shopkeepers bedding down for the night.

# Fifteen
# Johore Zoo

There's no doubt that Johore Zoo had to be one of the worst zoos in the world. Many of the cages were cramped, most of the animals, if not all, were unhappy and the whole place stank to high heaven. From the three legged tiger to the gorilla clapping for food in his small prison, you couldn't help feeling sorry for the animals. Yet, at the time, it was incredibly popular and as kids, we all loved going there.

The Daley family at Johore Zoo.

The zoo was built in 1928 by Sultan Sir Ibrahim. It was handed over to the government to manage in the early 1960s and it was opened to the public in 1962.It's still there today and has many visitors though reports in the local newspapers would suggest that conditions for the animals haven't changed much in 40 years!

# Sixteen
# Kota Tinghi Waterfalls

Kota Tinghi Waterfalls were situated at Lombong to the North East of Johore Bahru. We all enjoyed going there and it was a popular destination for Forces personnel and their families. People would enjoy swimming around the base of the falls which were located at the bottom of Gunung Muntahak mountain. The cool river ran into a series of pools that were ideal for bathing.

The Daley family approaching Kota Tinghi Falls in April 1967.

**Kevin Daley remembers: Kota Tinghi Waterfalls 1967. This was our first time here and in no time we were in the swimming pool area of the river.**

Me at the waterfalls looking like I've just discovered something!

Me with my mum and dad.

Kota Tinghi Waterfalls 1967.

**Kevin Daley remembers: It was on the rocks of the waterfall that Ray and I first saw giant black ants. They were well over an inch long.**

My brother, Alan, with the waterfalls in the background. There are a few people swimming to the left. I notice that my brother has his Kodak Brownie camera with him and he probably took some of the photos here of our family.

The bottom of the falls. This photo shows how busy the falls were at times not only with the families of service personnel but also with locals.

The Daley family at Kota Tinghi Waterfalls, 1967. I don't remember it being this busy when we visited.

My dad with his cine camera at the waterfalls.

# Seventeen
# Jason's Bay

The Daley family off to Jason's Bay on New Year's Day 1967.

The Daley family at Jason's Bay with a much needed sun awning.

**Ellen Tait remembers:**
**We loved going to Jason's Bay. A few families would drive there and we'd put up the parachute, attached to each car to provide shade. We all had fun in the sea, playing ball games and having the usual barbeque.**

Me and my brother in a boat made of sand at Jason's Bay. The shells spell 'Jasons' on the side.

The Daley family at Jason's Bay on New Year's Day 1967.

# Eighteen

# Around Malaya

A Kampong in the jungle 1961.

**Kevin Daley remembers:**
**I have already mentioned our close relationship with some of the**
**local children. Ray and I would often go off into the jungle with these**
**friends and they taught us some bush craft and kept an eye out for**
**us. They used to use the beds of rivers as walkways which were far**
**easier to navigate than trying to walk through the dense jungle.**
**We often headed through the jungle to pick up the railway line which**
**linked the north of Malaya with Singapore.**
**I recall one 'expedition' when we were told that there was not a**
**single snake that lived in the rivers that wasn't poisonous!**
**If my mother had any idea what Ray and I got up to, she would have**
**packed us off home to England!**
**For us, Malaya was one big adventure. A favourite haunt of ours was**
**in the jungle passed Jalan Merrawak. Next to the river was a large**
**area of blue and grey clay and during our first year in Malaya we**
**managed to divert some of the river water into a clay pit that we were**
**digging out with our friend, Alan West. We had made our own fresh**
**water swimming pool and unless it had rained and washed earth into**
**it, the water was always crystal clear.**
**It was the same road that used to flood during monsoon season and**
**we always headed down there to swim in the street. Ray had the**
**misfortune of being washed into one of the large monsoon drains at**

the end of the road and ultimately ended up in the river with all manner of frogs, insects and snakes.

We also used to head to the river bridge on the main north-south road and help to push vehicles through the deluge for 20 cents per car.

I am sure that anyone who lived in this area of the world will always remember the variety and, more impressively, the sheer size of the insects. There used to be an area of unmanaged ground near to our house in Jalan Giam. This is where I used to catch the largest moths in the world. These Atlas moths lived on the Tree of Heaven and the caterpillars were known as silkworms.

On my return from Malaya, I was still fascinated by insects and general flora and fauna. I have been a member of the British Entomological and Natural History Society for some years now and this all stems back to my childhood years, growing up in Malaya. You could say it is where I caught the bug!

During our trips into the jungle and elsewhere we always managed to find fruit that we could eat. Rambutans, bananas, smelly durian and many others were abundant. Our favourite thirst quencher was the crushed ice drinks that you could buy in and around JB. My mother didn't like us buying them as they were meant to be a real risk to health (I can imagine the lack of hygiene standards) but the flavoured ice, sultanas , melon and other bits of fruit really hit the spot.

Traditional Malay dancing.

Malayan Restaurant 1961.

**Kevin Daley remembers:**
I remember fishing the causeway. Ray and I often tried to fish from the causeway linking Singapore Island with JB. There were two memorable events that stick vividly in my mind.

If anyone ever walked along the waters edge of the causeway they will remember that there were a lot of quite large round concrete pipes running under the road at frequent intervals. They linked both sides of the straits and I assume it was to allow storm surges or significant differences in tidal heights to be released into the lower water level.

The whole length of the Skudai and causeway was infested with rats in epidemic proportions. As you will know, the Sweet Water Canal passed through JB's market and it was nothing short of an open sewer and a means of waste disposal. The outflow from the canal provided rich pickings for the rats, sea birds and other scavenging animals that roamed this area.

During one fishing trip, we were in a catching lull and our attention turned to the many rats that were clambering over the rocks and tucking into the trophies that littered the waters edge. At one point, we saw a large rat (cat size in Malaya) bouncing along the edge of the causeway, passing several of the entrances to the concrete pipes. As we continued to watch the rat getting closer to our own location, we were amazed to see a head of something lurch out from inside the hole and grab the rat with the inevitable squealing and commotion of a kill in action. Within a few seconds another section of the hunter appeared from within the tunnel and we saw it to be a large lizard. This wasn't anything like the Chit-Chats we were used to in our home. Far from it, this was a big lizard. It was in excess of 3 feet in length. Needless to say, our fishing trip to the Causeway came to an abrupt end. We later learnt that we had seen our first Monitor lizard, probably a Water Monitor.

The second 'event' to beset me on the causeway happened once again on a fishing trip. Ray and I were happily fishing away when we noticed a large group of local children heading our way from the Singapore side. In no time, they had scaled the barrier and were making a beeline for our location. We started to get a bit anxious and hastily started putting away our fishing gear. They started shouting at us and stated that they wanted the fishing rods and were going to take them. We started to hold our ground even though we were outnumbered. It was at this point that I was hit on the head by a large rock. My head hurt like hell and we decided our best option was to run as fast as we could to the customs station on the JB side. We escaped with our tackle intact and I was lucky to escape serious injury. With the recent Monitor episode and now a confrontation with the locals, we decided that the causeway was better off limits to our fishing ventures.

I have to say that bearing in mind we were a small minority amongst the local people, this event was the only one of hostility we encountered during our stay in Malaya.

On the whole, we were well treated and the majority of our friends were either Malay or of Chinese extraction. I later understood that things were a lot more remote for the people that lived on the Malayan peninsular than for those living on Singapore Island. In hindsight, I appreciated the remoteness we experience because I feel we touched and sampled the local culture a lot more than if we had lived at Singapore.

The Daley Family exploring the rubber plantation.

**Kevin Daley remembers:**
**So they cut a helix on the trunk at around a 30 degree angle. At the bottom of the cut they attached half of a small tin can. Each day they cut another helix, and so on.**
**Every 24 hours they'd tip out about 2 table spoons of latex which is white and very sticky.**
**I wonder how many cuts it took to make a set of tyres?**

The Daley family examining a rubber tree.

**Kevin Daley remembers:**
I joined the scouts during my time in Malaya and enjoyed every minute. The highlight for me was a week's camp away from home. We travelled way up north to an army camp in the back of 5 tonners. I remember seeing the biggest monsoon drains I had ever seen and commented on them. We were told that there were tigers in the area and the drains width formed the best protection. I never did know if this was true but I know it kept us all inside at lights-out. We were due to ride in a Wessex helicopter and ride in a Saracen armoured car. This would have been the highlight of the week. Unfortunately some older boys from another group kept mucking about and the leaders warned us that if any more misbehaviour occurred, the helicopter and armoured car trips would be cancelled. I was devastated and really annoyed when sure enough, the bad behaviour continued and I never did get to go up in the chopper.

The highlight of the week was a venture into the jungle with a member of the jungle warfare school. He showed us how to find water, what you could eat and what you had to stay clear of to survive.

An amazing experience as was my whole time in Malaya and Singapore.

# Nineteen
# Penang

Anyone who stayed at the Sandycroft Leave Centre will have fond memories of Penang. Who could forget the huge, yellow car ferry that took you across to Penang Island or the Penang Railway that took you high above the humidity of Georgetown? There were also the monkeys at the Botanic Gardens which we all enjoyed seeing.

I remember the time my dad hired a Toyota and drove us from our home at Johore Bahru to the Sandycroft Leave Centre. It seemed a very long journey. The petrol gauge didn't work and the car was so small that my dad had his knees up to his chest. There were lots of dead snakes on the road up which at first we thought were fan belts. This was the first time I remember being car sick. Stopping off to go to the toilet in a place which turned out to be where they killed chickens still sticks in my memory! Chickens really do still run around after their heads have been cut off. Anyway, we got there safely. We took the plane after that!

My mum on the Toyota trip to Penang. It was such a long journey, we were probably glad of the pit stop!

Here's a shot of the ferry terminal. I can't see my dad's car amongst the ones here though! After our long car journey, I'm sure we must have been very relieved by the time we got there, especially with the heat in the car. We certainly didn't have air conditioning! It's funny that I don't remember the journey back though.

It was certainly worth the travel and we had a great time once we were at Sandycroft. It was lovely being right by the sea and we'd explore while our parents were swimming, water skiing or playing cricket on the beach.

Apparently, when I was about three or so, my brother took me to see Born Free at the cinema there and I cried all the way through. I don't remember crying but I do remember seeing the film there so it must have happened!

Another shot of the ferry terminal.

The Butterworth Car Ferry from the mainland to Penang.

**John Cunningham remembers the Butterworth Ferry:**
**The big yellow ferry boat is still there and I remember when we**
**crossed once, we came across some unfortunate soul who was**
**floating face down in the water. We were told it wasn't unusual, mind**
**you it certainly sobered you up!**

This photo shows a Coca Cola seller selling his wares from what looks like a hand cart made out of old bicycles. Who could forget the long gone classic shape of a glass Coca-Cola bottle? As well as Coke, they always seemed to sell bags of popcorn as well.

Here's a great shot of the Penang Railway. It seemed wonderful going up such a steep incline and being able to see way over Penang and all the surrounding jungle.

**David Yap remembers:**
**One particular place full of memories is Penang Hill as my father was in the Civil Service and we used to stay in the Government chalets. One such house was by the top rail station. A great topic back then was that some of these houses were haunted, though I never had an encounter!**

Richard Freeman and his sister feeding the monkeys at Penang's
Botanical Gardens.

I have to admit to being scared of the monkeys at the Botanic Gardens in
Penang. At the time though, I probably didn't feel like I was much bigger
than them! We would take bananas in for them which I would keep behind
my back but it wouldn't be long before one of them had crept up and
snatched the lot!. With it being so humid, everyone left their car windows
down which often meant that you'd return and find a load of monkeys in
your car that you had to shoo off. It could be worse though, sometimes
they left something behind!

The monkeys were everywhere and if you had any food at all, they were
sure to gather. It made having a picnic pretty interesting.

Here's a photo of me at the Sandycroft Leave Centre. I look excited to be there or perhaps there was a huge jellyfish approaching.

I don't remember who this dog belonged to but it followed us everywhere while we were staying at Sandycroft. I do remember his name was Pepper though. I probably wanted to take him back home!

My mum and brother at Sandycroft. This area has changed quite a bit since the 1960s and there are now even a few high rise blocks casting shadows on the beach.

My mum in the pool at Sandycroft in about 1965.

# Twenty
# Christmas

Christmas was a wonderful time in Singapore and Malaya. The build up to it was fantastic, putting up all the decorations and decorating the tree even though there was a heat wave outside. There was nothing like the amazing toys you got in Singapore at the time and a trip to Tang's at Christmas was an experience in itself. Also, there was the Naval Party to look forward to at the Woodlands Base, along with the presents and firework displays. Some of my best Christmas's were spent in Singapore and Malaya and I still remember the excitement of getting up on Christmas morning, especially the year I got a go-kart!
No doubt everyone will remember the great toys we got. From battery operated tin robots to pedal cars, bikes and all manner of toys.

**Kevin Daley remembers:**
**Our first Xmas in Malaya. You almost imagine ice and snow and cold to be associated with Christmas time. We even went to the beach on one Christmas Day. Cool.**

The Daley family. Christmas Dinner 1966.

**Kevin Daley remembers:**
**The interesting thing I noticed about our Xmas pictures is the lack of
decorations. Apart from the false tree and cards, here and there, you
wouldn't know it was at the height of the festive season. I can only
think that hanging decorations were hard to come by or was it that
we were respecting the fact that a high proportion of the population
were Muslim?**

My brother and me decorating the Christmas tree. As you can see, it was
a bit warmer there than it is in England in December!

189

Christmas Panto 1959.

**Claire Carter remembers:**
**My Dad was Lt Williamson and used to be Father Christmas at the children's party at the wardroom at KD Malaya in the 1960s. He used to arrive in a MGB sports car driven by Batman!**

I remember the Father Christmas at KD Malaya well. I think I remember him getting out of a helicopter one year. All the kids would get excited because he was coming and we'd all get a gift. Mine was a camera, I think it fell apart when we got home! There would also be a party laid on for all the kids and there would be lots of food. I'm not sure if the party was actually on Christmas Day or not as I remember being at our home in Malaya on the actual day.

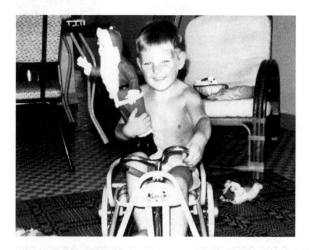

Me on Christmas Day with my new go kart and a waving Santa.

Naval Base Police Christmas party 1956.
In the background are the flats at the top of Ottawa Road. Some of the people in the picture are Deanna and Christine Morton, Karen Brooking, Susan Rainey and Roxanne Wilcox.

At the RN school December 1957 .
Deanna Morton is the dragon, with Geoffrey Hammond facing her with a cushion stuffed up his jumper and Patricia Alison is the tall girl, back left. Richard White is the guard with a shield on the far left of the photo.

191

Two photos of the Nativity Play at Kebunteh School in Malaya, 1960s.
I remember the Nativity Plays well at Kebunteh. I'm sure that I even took part in one.

**Kevin Daley remembers:**
**I remember the Santa at the senior rates mess in Singapore. My memory is a lot clearer with the Gully Gully man though who always dropped by the house on Christmas day. He would do tricks and charm snakes. We had Christmas on the beach at Jason's Bay one year. And I also remember having my haircut sat on a chair in the front garden. Christmas was different in a tropical climate.**

## Twenty One
# Heading Home

Heading home was a culture shock. After three years or more living in the Far East, you had to get used to a new home and a new school. And, if you were travelling back to Britain, you also had to get used to the cold and wet climate. We flew back home and I remember stopping in Nicosia, Cyprus on the way back to refuel. I never thought at the time that it would be another thirty years before I would return to Singapore.

We all look back on living in Singapore and Malaya with fond memories. It seems a lifetime ago now and I wouldn't be surprised if many of us would happily return to those times if we were given a choice.

Peter Banks, homeward bound.

**John Harper remembers:**
**At the end of the summer term, we were scheduled to return to the UK just as the term finished. We were supposed to be returning on the SS Nevassa, a slightly newer ship than the Dilwara that we had come out to Singapore on. I recall seeing the ship coming into harbour and thinking, 'I'll be on that the day after tomorrow!'. Unfortunately, it was not to be. My father came down with a bad bout of influenza and was quickly followed by my two brothers. This meant our leaving was delayed and we ended up flying home from**

193

**Paya Lebar airport on a Hunting Clan Britannia turbo jet. This was another first for me, flying in an aeroplane. It was so memorable for me that I can remember the registration of the aircraft as G-APNB. The other thing that is memorable is that this was the last aircraft that my father ever flew in and it was duly noted down in his flying log which he had kept up to date since ferrying aircraft across the Atlantic during World War II.**

Paya Lebar airport 1960s.

**Tim Ecott remembers:**
**We came back to England on the SS Chitral and called at Ceylon, Durban, Cape Town, Gibraltar, Lisbon and Le Havre. Coming back to Britain was a huge shock for us all and I almost lost my love for swimming when confronted with an unheated open air pool!**

So, there we have it! Most of us survived our time in the Far East and made it back home to the cold and wet climate, in my case, of England. I'm sure that most of us would never have an experience like it again and I'm sure there's not one of us that doesn't miss it.
I hope this book has rekindled all those happy memories and, don't worry, there's still lots more memories and photos to fill another book!